The Gateway Arch soars 630 feet in a graceful curve which seems to reach for the sky.

The achievements of the designers and builders of the Arch mirror those of the explorers, traders, and settlers who lived in the American West, which the Arch commemorates.

THE GATEWAY ARCH

AN ARCHITECTURAL DREAM

TEXT BY ROBERT J. MOORE, JR.

ORAL AND WRITTEN ESSAYS EDITED BY ROBERT J. MOORE, JR.

Published by

JEFFERSON
NATIONAL PARKS
ASSOCIATION

OUR MISSION:
To educate and inspire present and future generations
through the priceless national parks and historic treasures
of St. Louis and the nation.

ISBN 0-931056-24-1 (Hardcover)
ISBN 0-931056-25-x (Limited Edition)

Text by Robert J. Moore, Jr.

Production and Editorial Support by
Joseph M. Luman & Richard T. Trigg

Graphic Design by
David Katz & Chad Combs © Terrell Creative

Art Direction by
Chad Combs & William D. Eichler

Designed in the United States of America by

Terrell Creative

Printed in China

Library of Congress Control Number: 2005924749

INTRODUCTION

George B. Hartzog, Jr.,
Director, National Park Service, 1964-1972

"Y OU must be losing your mind," a colleague remarked on hearing I was to be the new superintendent of the Jefferson National Expansion Memorial in St. Louis. Among Park Service careerists, "JNEM," as it is generally called, was not a preferred assignment.

Contrariwise, it was the first national historic site established after passage of the Historic Sites Act of 1935, and it had such a great story to tell. Occupying a bluff above the Mississippi River, it was, figuratively, a gateway used by explorers like Lewis and Clark, Pike, Long and Fremont, the mountain men of the fur trade era, eager seekers of gold in California, and the homesteaders in covered wagons bound for Oregon.

When I arrived in St. Louis in January 1959, work was just beginning to relocate railroad tracks on the levee, which separated the site from the Mississippi River, by placing them in an underground tunnel. Only then could construction begin on the Gateway Arch, a massive architectural and engineering challenge that many

doubted could be accomplished. The memorial site itself was composed of 37 city blocks along the river, from which all structures had been removed prior to World War II. A part of this vacant space served as a city parking lot. To say the least, the job seemed like a daunting one, to build an important national memorial from literally nothing. My job was to ensure that one of the world's most recognizable structures would rise from a weed-filled no man's land.

My background would not seem to have prepared me for the complications ahead. I was a country lawyer from a small town in South Carolina whose formal education began in a one-room schoolhouse. Without the benefit of college or law school I passed the bar examination by reading law, as I like to point out, just as Abraham Lincoln had done. With the help of a lawyer friend from my army experience in World War II, I joined the Park Service in 1946. Before coming to JNEM, I was assigned to be assistant superintendent at Rocky Mountain and then at Great Smoky Mountains National Park.

When I arrived at JNEM, I found the construction program, then underway, enormously complicated, perhaps because the interests of more than two dozen federal, state, and city agencies were involved. For example, the U.S. Army Corps of Engineers held jurisdiction over our construction on the riverfront, and the City of St. Louis was especially concerned not only because we were disturbing its roads and bridges, but because the city contributed one dollar to every three dollars of federal money needed for development.

I remember with warmth and gratitude the support I received from St. Louis Mayor Raymond Tucker, who was previously an engineering professor. Unlike, perhaps, many mayors, he was charismatic, smart as a whip and organized. "You move the paper," he would say, "I'll handle the politics."

But the most notable figure in the development of the memorial was the architect, Eero Saarinen. He was a genius, reserved but not introverted, brilliant but not bookish, demanding of others but not bullying. I found him always approachable, and willing to take suggestions - except, of course, on matters of design. In that area he was like a block of granite.

In my view, his Gateway Arch is, along with the Washington Monument, one of our grandest architectural memorials. The art critic for the *New York Times*, Aline Louchheim, who later became Eero's second wife, best described the Gateway Arch, calling it "timeless, but of our time." It is indeed timeless. When I think of my years at JNEM, time stands still for me as well. The challenges were great, but the rewards were worth every effort. By the time the Arch was completed I was the director of the National Park Service in Washington, a position

from which I could ensure the memorial's completion, despite the efforts of naysayers and doubting Thomases.

Unfortunately, Eero Saarinen, that brilliant genius, died in 1961, and never saw one bit of that Arch built. Many years later, when I was out there in the evening, at dusk, when the lights were beginning to show on the sides of the Arch, I thought, "Eero, I wish you were here." But I'm sure he is there in spirit. And like the Arch, his spirit makes the hearts, minds, and imaginations of all who visit that place soar toward the sky, like the transcendent dream of the Arch itself.

A gleeful George Hartzog receives a check for $500,000 from the Terminal Railroad Association on July 16, 1959. The funds represented the Terminal Railroad Association's contribution for relocating the railroad tracks and signaled the start of the construction of the memorial. From left to right: Sidney Maestre, Chairman of the Board of the Mercantile Trust Company; Gregory Maxwell, President of the Terminal Railroad Association; JNEM Superintendent George B. Hartzog, Jr.; and St. Louis Mayor Raymond R. Tucker.

THE ARCH AT 40 YEARS
Fran P. Mainella,
Director, National Park Service

ONE of the dedicated walkers and runners of the Gateway Arch grounds (of which there are many), once described the soaring, stainless steel memorial as giving the appearance of "a giant striding into the future." This description seems to summarize the feeling a human being has when visiting the Gateway Arch. It is bigger than life. It changes its appearance with the weather, time of day, and the seasons. It is a unique symbol, seen in different ways by different people, and used - most of all used. The Arch is local, national, and international all at one time.

As Director of the National Park Service, it has been my privilege to make several visits to the Gateway Arch. Aside from its visual beauty, I think the thing that has impressed me the most about it is that it draws people to it, who in turn interact with one another on its spacious, breezy grounds and within the recesses of the underground visitor center and museum complex. During that interaction they learn about our nation, its culture, its past, and perhaps something about themselves.

The Jefferson National Expansion Memorial, which is the official name of the park that includes the Gateway Arch, is a prime example of a park engineered to fit into an existing urban environment. An afterthought as far as city planning goes, the park provides a dramatic respite from a congested inner-city area, opening up the riverfront and the crowded towers of the downtown area to sunlight and spacious vistas. The park also provides a stage on which the National Park Service message can be presented to an urban audience.

For a lot of people the traditional image of the National Park Service employee is of someone wearing a "Smokey Bear" hat hiking through the wilderness or staffing some remote post in a place where nature has outdone itself in creating a magnificent setting. But the National Park Service also includes many of our nation's great historical and cultural treasures. As we move into the 21st century, and our nation becomes more and more urbanized, it is imperative that our citizens, especially the younger generation, are made aware of the full scope of these resources, and that the National Park Service is the caretaker of many of these special places.

One more thing that I admire about the Gateway Arch is its lengthy legacy of public-private partnerships. From the earliest years of its establishment in 1935, the park has provided a fine example of ways in which organizations and individuals in the private sector can be instrumental in the administration of a National Park Service area. Even the money that built the Arch came through a partnership of federal and city funds. Today, the assistance rendered to the park by the Jefferson National Parks Association, which manages the park's museum stores, and Metro, which runs the trams that take people to the top of the Arch, as well as the interpretive riverboat cruises along the St. Louis riverfront, is so important that the park truly could not function without these vital park partners.

Just as Jefferson National Expansion Memorial fosters an awareness and a sense of pride in the accomplishments of the people who inhabited, explored and settled the American West, the Gateway Arch inspires its visitors and the people who work there with the potential and possibilities inherent in our national parks. Like a giant striding into the future, the Arch moves us all toward new frontiers of education, interaction, preservation, and partnership within the urban grid.

* * * *

A Note from the Superintendent
Peggy O'Dell,
Superintendent, Jefferson National Expansion Memorial

COMING home. What a great set of images that conjured up in my mind when I heard in December, 2003 that I had been selected as the Superintendent of Jefferson National Expansion Memorial. I remembered so fondly my first job for the National Park Service as a seasonal park ranger at the Arch during my summer break from college in the early 1970s. It was such an exciting place to work, with 25,000 visitors a day and a staff made up of seasoned professionals and young, energetic students who took such pride in providing public service. The pace was hectic, the park visitors interesting and the friendships we made lasted a lifetime. I was so proud to work at a site that belongs to the American people and is a world-renowned symbol of my hometown.

As I sit in my office today and look out over this magnificent National Memorial, I still feel blessed to have this career in public service. To be a witness to the changes made to the facility since those early days is a remarkable experience. The National Park Service and our partners at Jefferson National Parks Association and Metro have invested 40 years to develop a premier program of educational opportunities and visitor services creating cherished memories for more than 100 million visitors since the Arch opened in 1967.

I look forward to working with our community to create the next generation of leadership for St. Louis and the Arch, equaling the vision of those who saw a monument rise from the St. Louis riverfront. Please join us in celebrating our past and envisioning our future. The Gateway Arch, 40 years of inspiring monumental dreams – a great idea to come home to.

The restored St. Louis Courthouse, built between 1839 and 1862, became part of Jefferson National Expansion Memorial in 1940. The "Old Courthouse," as it later became known, was where two slaves, Dred Scott and his wife Harriet, sued for their freedom in 1846. Their case, which was finally decided by an infamous Supreme Court opinion in 1857, helped touch off the Civil War.

CHAPTER 1

THE MEMORIAL IDEA IS BORN

1935-1947

A MEMORIAL IS CREATED
Hon. Thomas Eagleton,
U.S. Senator (D-MO), (1968-87)

JEFFERSON National Expansion Memorial was the brainchild of Luther Ely Smith, a prominent St. Louis attorney. The project was non-partisan from the start. Smith was a Republican, but he convinced the Democratic mayor of St. Louis, Bernard Dickmann, that a riverfront memorial honoring the western territorial expansion of the United States, particularly President Thomas Jefferson, should be built. Smith formed a committee which included Dickmann and other powerful and civic-minded St. Louisans such as Morton "Buster" May, and they obtained a state charter in 1934 as the nonprofit Jefferson National Expansion Memorial Association.

At first, Smith and Dickmann asked the federal government for $30 million to build the memorial, in two separate bills drafted in 1934. This was a blunder, for during the Great Depression a request for such a large sum was considered in the larger context of the suffering nation. Smith backed off, and two new bills were introduced which called only for the creation of a Federal Memorial Commission. Despite heavy opposition, especially in the U.S. Senate, the bill authorizing a 15-member memorial commission passed and was signed by President Franklin D. Roosevelt on June 15, 1934.

On July 1, 1935, the St. Louis Board of Aldermen passed an ordinance permitting a special bond issue election to contribute $7.5 million toward the memorial. On September 10, the people of St. Louis voted on the measure. It was a controversial issue, with well-organized and vocal adherents on both sides of the question. The proposal passed 123,299 to 50,713, these figures representing a huge voter turnout. But many challenged the validity of the election, and landowners in the memorial area fought the acquisition of their property in court battles. In addition, although Smith had expected the federal government to step into the project at some point, Attorney General Homer Cummings announced that he did not feel that the government could legally support the establishment and construction of a memorial in St. Louis.

Mayor Dickmann took the train to Washington, and made an appointment to see Cummings. Dickmann said that he wanted Cummings to think as the Democratic National Committee Chairman, and not as the Attorney General. When Cummings said that there would be no funding for the memorial, Dickmann is said to have responded that he wanted Cummings to take a message to Roosevelt; that the President was going to be running for a second term, and if St. Louis could not get the funds, Dickmann would personally lead the fight against FDR's reelection in Missouri. This was no idle threat, for Dickmann was, along with Bob Hannegan, one of the two most powerful Democratic political bosses in the eastern half of the state of Missouri. It was at this point that Cummings fell back on a recently created law, the Historic Sites Act, which he used to authorize the creation of Jefferson National Expansion Memorial. On December 21, 1935, President Roosevelt signed an executive order creating the memorial, which was to be administered by the National Park Service.

(Opposite page) By the early 1930s the once bustling St. Louis riverfront district had been bypassed and suffered from blight and neglect. Even as early as 1874, Mark Twain, who had been a riverboat pilot in the heyday of the trade prior to the Civil War, was prompted to write that he saw "half a dozen sound asleep steamboats where I used to see a solid mile of wide-awake ones! This was melancholy, this was woeful. The absence of the pervading and jocund steamboatman from the billiard-saloon was explained. He was absent because he was no more."

(Top) By the early 1930s the riverfront was dominated by a large train trestle that ran between the old buildings and the river. The first sight that greeted visitors to St. Louis was the forlorn-looking trestle and the crumbling, sleepy riverfront.

(Bottom) St. Louis lawyer Luther Ely Smith saw a scene very similar to this when he returned to the city by train after attending the dedication of the George Rogers Clark Memorial in Vincennes, Indiana in 1933. The view spurred him to challenge the city to aspire to greater things and beautify its "front porch" with a memorial to westward expansion.

Jefferson National Expansion Memorial, and the Gateway Arch which is its centerpiece, is an unusual National Park Service site. Its origins were equally out of the ordinary. The idea for the park was generated in the early 1930s by a bespectacled, middle-aged lawyer and self-proclaimed "do-gooder" named Luther Ely Smith, who wanted to beautify the run-down St. Louis riverfront. In the era before commercial aviation was common, the riverfront area was the first glimpse those in automobiles and trains had as they approached the city. It was not a pretty sight, and did not make visitors think that St. Louis was one of the great American cities. In addition to beautifying the city, Smith also wanted to put St. Louisans back to work during the Great Depression. Also, Smith wanted their efforts to result in a unique memorial which would draw tourists from all over the world. The memorial would commemorate a legitimate landmark in U.S. history - the unprecedented migration during the 19th century of hundreds of thousands of people into the trans-Mississippi West, funneled through the bustling city of St. Louis, the last major metropolitan center on the edge of the frontier. Although revitalizing the riverfront was not a new idea (proposals had been made as far back as 1898), Smith had the reputation and dedication to push his own concept to reality.

Although some political arm-twisting was needed to make the project come to fruition, without the passion of its early backers, the memorial – and the Arch – would never have come to be. It was just the beginning of a lot of hard work, dedication, and unusual twists and turns applied over a period of 30 years, which made the memorial project a reality.

Franklin D. Roosevelt, who created Jefferson National Expansion Memorial with an executive order on December 21, 1935, visited the area of the park on October 14, 1936. Here Franklin and Eleanor Roosevelt are seen touring the site from a car being driven along the levee near the railroad trestle. St. Louis Mayor Bernard Dickmann sits immediately in front of the president.

LUTHER ELY SMITH:
FOUNDER OF A MEMORIAL
Christine Ely Smith,
Granddaughter of Luther Ely Smith

M Y grandfather, Luther Ely Smith, had the vision and the perseverance that made the Gateway Arch a reality, despite what often seemed to be insurmountable obstacles. He was a quiet man who did not seek the limelight, but he was persuasive and innovative. Breakfast meetings at his home were his solution to people who were too busy to meet with him for lunch. People might be "too busy" to meet for lunch, but who has appointments at seven in the morning?

In 1933, on his way back into St. Louis on the train after the dedication of the George Rogers Clark Memorial at Vincennes, Indiana, my grandfather once again saw the deteriorating St. Louis riverfront and decided that there should be a memorial to westward expansion there instead. It should be educational and it should become the true heart of the city.

With the help of St. Louis architect Louis La Beaume, a neighbor, a national competition was planned to choose a design for the memorial. While Smith was raising the $225,000 needed for the competition, he went back to one of his large donors to ask for more money. The donor's response was "I already gave you some money," but my grandfather said, "Now you have to protect your investment." Still $40,000 shy of his goal in 1946, he personally underwrote the balance.

Despite the Great Depression, World War II, and the Korean conflict, tenacity and gentle persuasiveness brought the Arch to reality. I believe that the riverfront memorial has become what my grandfather envisioned when he rode that train into town in 1933. He felt that there should be a central feature, a shaft, a building, an arch, or something which would symbolize American culture and civilization. He loved the concept of the Arch when he saw it in 1948. It truly was and is, in his words, "transcending in spiritual and aesthetic values." It has firmly anchored the heart of St. Louis to the riverfront, and brings attention

to the importance of the city and Thomas Jefferson in the story of the nation's westward expansion.

Although my grandfather died in April of 1951, and never saw the Arch completed, he would have been proud to see that the park created green space along the river (he was an avid birder and conservationist), and that the museum provides wonderful educational opportunities. Because of his vision and his belief that if someone doesn't agree with you, you haven't explained yourself well enough, St. Louis has a memorial that attracts millions of visitors each year from the world over and a symbol that is recognized worldwide. When he died the *St. Louis Globe-Democrat* wrote: "Those who are calling for a revival in public morals need not search long for an example of the good man. They need only hold up the life of Luther Ely Smith."

The quiet streets of the riverfront region would soon be transformed by the vision of one man – Luther Ely Smith. The Old Rock House, then the oldest building in St. Louis, can be seen just beyond the trestle on the left. Built in 1818 by fur trapper Manuel Lisa, the building had been used as a warehouse for furs, a sail loft to make covers for pioneer wagons, and a tavern known for the boisterous songs of "Rock House Annie" in the 1930s.

In a ceremony attended by Luther Ely Smith on October 10, 1939, Mayor Bernard Dickmann inaugurated the memorial project when he pried three bricks loose from a building at 7 Market Street. The city preserved the first brick, while Dickmann sent the second to President Roosevelt. The third brick was given to an enthusiastic young man in the crowd. Demolition of the buildings in the riverfront area followed in a three-year project.

*O*nce the land for the memorial was acquired, the first tasks of the National Park Service involved setting up an office, studying the historical events that took place in old St. Louis which were the basis of the creation of the park, and razing all of the buildings in the riverfront district, a total of 37 square blocks, to make room for the as-yet undesigned memorial. Although many of these buildings were in bad condition, some were also historical and architectural treasures - their wholesale demolition between 1939 and 1942 continues to rankle preservationists to this day. Only three buildings were preserved: the Old Courthouse (built 1839-1862 and the site of the first Dred Scott trials), the Old Cathedral (built 1832-1834), and the Old Rock House, a fur trade warehouse built by Manuel Lisa in 1818, which was then the oldest standing building in St. Louis. The Old Rock House was torn down in 1959 to make way for the railroad relocation project as the Arch was built; portions of this structure are on display in exhibit areas in the Old Courthouse.

BEGINNING WORK ON THE MEMORIAL
Charles E. Peterson,
Historical Architect with the National Park
Service, Founder of the Historic American
Buildings Survey

I started with the National Park Service in 1929 after taking a civil service examination for landscape architect, and after six months I entered on duty in San Francisco, after which I was sent East to help start some new projects, especially at George Washington's Birthplace in Virginia. After working at Colonial National Historical Park I was brought to Washington in 1933, and then the St. Louis project came up in 1936.

We set up office in the Buder Building at 7th and Market Streets in St. Louis, sitting on packing boxes until the furniture came in. Superintendent John Nagle rented the space and ordered the goods. Nagle had been the civilian head engineer on the Arlington Memorial Bridge. He was a very bright, and a very unusual chap, something of an intellectual, as a matter of fact, which is not common among engineers, even the bright ones. The first time the staff met, and this is very clear in my memory, Nagle said to the engineers, "I want you fellows to know more about this piece of land that we are acquiring than anybody else in the world." And since I was interested in historic sites and buildings, that's all I needed to know, and I took off on a study of the French that had built the place.

It was assumed that the area would be cleared out. They had no thought about saving anything. Even the Cathedral was to be moved, and put across the street. We in the Park Service were supposed to be in the business of saving buildings, and here we were pulling them down, and wholesale! It was the biggest demolition the Park Service ever had. Nobody had any thought about saving it. But that was on account of the times – we live in a different atmosphere now. I tried like mad to save some of those buildings. We had a plan for the landscape of the park, and proposed two museums. One was a museum of the fur trade, the other of American architecture. We took down four whole cast-iron facades, unscrewing them carefully. They would have faced inward and composed the courtyard of the Museum of Architecture.

We worked on the Old Courthouse after the Park Service acquired it in 1940. First we did the roof over. The roof was originally copper, and I wanted it copper again, but the engineers had heard that lead-coated copper was even better, so they put that on over my protests. It turns a different color when it's weathered. The roof trusses were very early wrought-iron trusses, too, and they cut them out and threw them away.

When the war came along, it ended my direct association with the project in St. Louis. I volunteered for the Civil Engineer

In 1939 the Old Courthouse looked shabby, as seen in the upper picture. Covered in black soot from coal dust and suffering from neglect, the 1839-1862 structure received a face-lift from the National Park Service. The City of St. Louis deeded the structure to the federal government in 1940, and by 1942 (bottom) the building had a new roof and had been cleaned and painted.

The Old Cathedral, surrounded and engulfed by neighboring buildings in 1939, would emerge as the memorial grounds were cleared and once more be admired for its 1834 architecture. The Cathedral, now the Basilica of St. Louis, King of France, is the fourth building to stand on the site, and has been home to an active Roman Catholic parish since 1770.

Corps in the Navy, and I went to Washington in December, two days after Pearl Harbor. When my commission came through, I was posted to Admiral Nimitz's staff, where I was in charge of advance base engineering. I made plans for all the places the Seabees went in, from Guam clear to Tokyo.

In my opinion, the worst failure of the memorial was losing the Rock House and the whole collection of architectural fragments, which would have gone into the Museum of Architecture. The greatest triumph was that the Cathedral is still on its original site, and that the Old Courthouse was included in the park.

RAZING THE BUILDINGS IN THE MEMORIAL AREA
Howard Gruber, Engineer, National Park Service

(Top) By 1943 the Old Rock House had been extensively rebuilt and restored to its 1818 appearance. The restoration work on the reroofed building, which had a mid-19th century third story removed, included reconstruction of much of the rubble stone walls. This incarnation of the Rock House was dismantled in 1959 to make way for the railroad tunnel between the river and the Arch. Portions of the structure can still be viewed in exhibit areas in the Old Courthouse.

(Bottom) An idea of the amount of rubble and debris generated by the destruction of 40 blocks of structures can be gained from this photograph, taken in 1940. Most of the demolition work was documented in photographs, including the appearance of each of the buildings before it was razed; this photograph is now stored in the JNEM Archives.

I was one of the engineers responsible for the demolition of the riverfront buildings between 1939 and 1942. Prior to demolition there were several teams of us who went out in pairs and visited each building in the area where the memorial was to be built. We took structural notes on the building; the type of façade (many of them were cast iron), the size of the building, the number of floors, and type of construction, which were used by some people in the office to determine the value of the buildings. After we had surveyed all the buildings, I was out in the field working with the contractor who was tearing them down.

The foundations of the buildings were left in place. All the masonry and nondegradable parts of the buildings were put in the basements. If there was a slab in the basement of the building, the slabs were broken, and actually pried up, so there were no pockets of water kept throughout the area. Only masonry-type refuse was permitted in the backfill, although I'm not naive enough to think that that's all that went in there, because we couldn't watch the work all over the place. In one case I remember there was a 4' by 4' safe just laying in the rubble. One Monday morning, in fact, it was gone. And they assured me that they had taken it away. I requested that they dig where the safe was, and sure enough they found it about two feet under the rubble!

The riverfront district was built on the site of the original fur trading post of St. Louis as it was laid out by the French in 1764. With the removal of the primarily late 19th-century buildings from the area, the original street grid could be seen once again in a way no one had seen it in over 170 years. An idea of the topography of the site can be gained from this photo, which shows the gradual incline of the property toward the river, and the remnants of the original steep bluff fronting the water (on the left).

So I wouldn't be surprised at anything that might be found in there. Everything like that we tried to keep out.

The contractor, before they started wrecking a block, made an effort to determine if there was a keystone building in that block, that was in effect holding up the other buildings. If they tore that one down first, several of them might collapse, and result in some injuries. So they had to work around that and tear that keystone building down last. There were a couple of occasions when some buildings collapsed, although I don't remember any serious injuries. There were several different crews working at the same time. The buildings, generally speaking, were in pretty bad shape. There were some good ones, but there were more bad

ones. After the idea for the memorial came up and progressed, the owners of these buildings performed minimal maintenance in occupied buildings and none in the empty ones. There were literally hundreds of buildings. We photographed every building in the area. And every building had a sheet that had all the details of the structure; the size of the building, the number of floors, the type of interior construction, the type of façade.

After the work was completed we worked on the Old Courthouse, and shored up the ceilings of some of the court rooms, but in effect the whole area was shut down soon after Pearl Harbor. It was not essential during the time of the war.

22

(Top) The cleared memorial area can be seen in this aerial view, taken about 1942. A large warehouse was left standing on the southern portion of the memorial (seen in the center of this photo). It was used to house architectural fragments salvaged from the riverfront buildings, and torn down in 1959. The Old Cathedral and Old Rock House can also be seen near the center of the photograph.

(Bottom) During the 1930s the National Park Service's architectural and historical team, led by Charles E. Peterson, developed a plan for the memorial they called "Plan 8009." A plasticine model of the plan, seen in this photo, was created to explain their ideas. Plan 8009 had a central feature, an obelisk-like tower and several museum buildings set within the preserved grid of the original street plan. An ambitious vision with a sensitivity to the historic scene, Plan 8009 was nonetheless not what the city fathers and visionaries who created the memorial wanted JNEM to look like. Something more audacious and daring could only come, they felt, from an architectural competition.

CHAPTER 2

THE MEMORIAL COMPETITION

1947-1948

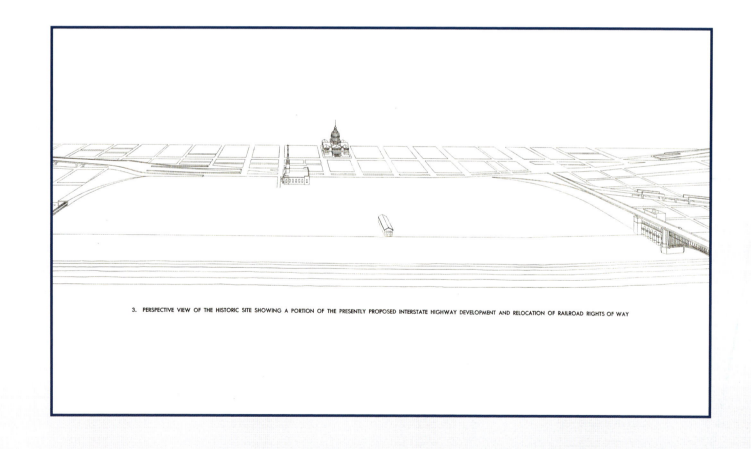

3.   PERSPECTIVE VIEW OF THE HISTORIC SITE SHOWING A PORTION OF THE PRESENTLY PROPOSED INTERSTATE HIGHWAY DEVELOPMENT AND RELOCATION OF RAILROAD RIGHTS OF WAY

The Second World War involved nearly every human being in the United States in some capacity during over four and a half years of conflict in Europe and in Asia. It was a huge effort of money, time, munitions, equipment, personnel, and sacrifice that disrupted the flow of everyday life for Americans. Thus it was not until two years after the war was successfully concluded that Luther Ely Smith could once more revitalize the memorial idea in St. Louis. During the war the riverfront district sat, a flat, empty 90-acre tract devoid of nearly any structure. Federal money was diverted to winning the war, and dusty winds blew through the deserted area.

After the war, money was privately raised for an architectural competition, which was formally announced in 1947. Entries were welcome from any architect who was an American citizen. It was the intent of the Jefferson National Expansion Memorial Association that the memorial area would become an integral part of the community's life, and revive the beauty and overall impression of the adjacent downtown area. Accordingly, five primary concerns were to be addressed in each competition proposal, as defined in the competition booklet developed by St. Louis architect Louis Le Beaume: the building of an architectural memorial; the preservation of the site of old St. Louis through a museum; the creation of a living memorial to Thomas Jefferson; the relocation of the unsightly riverfront railroad tracks; and a provision for an anticipated interstate highway.

In the immediate postwar era, with the emergence of the United States as the most prosperous and powerful of the industrialized nations, anything seemed possible. An American, Chuck Yeager, broke the sound barrier in 1947, and the nation looked toward rockets and jet aircraft to supplement plentiful food, labor-saving devices, affordable automobiles, television, and a cornucopia of consumer goods. Likewise, the view of architecture was seen to be full of limitless possibilities. The modern style of architecture, pioneered by Frank Lloyd Wright, Le Corbusier, Ludwig Mies van der Rohe, and others, had developed into the "international" style. The architects who approached the St. Louis memorial project thus had a free rein in terms of concept, use of materials, and the idea of what a memorial should be.

The competition was held in two stages, and judged by a jury of seven nationally recognized architects which included George Howe, William Wurster and Richard Neutra. The jury was predisposed toward the modern style of architecture, causing most of the entrants to take a modern rather than a classical, Bauhaus, Beaux Arts or other approach to the design. It was the first large competition held after World War II and the largest in terms of prize money – a total of $225,000 – ever held up to that point in time. So the competition had no trouble in drawing entrants from all over the United States, including big names like Walter Gropius, Eliel Saarinen, Charles Eames, Skidmore, Owings and Merrill, Louis Kahn, Eugene Mackey, Edward D. Stone, and Kazumi Adachi. A total of 172 entries were received. One young architect, 38-year old Eero Saarinen, after years of working for his father's firm, decided to enter the St. Louis competition with his own design team, which included his wife Lily Saarinen (a sculptor and artist), landscape architect Dan Kiley, illustrator J. Henderson Barr, and designer Alexander Girard.

(Opposite page) The centerfold spread from the 1947 JNEM Competition Booklet featured a blank space showing the St. Louis riverfront and the area of the proposed memorial. Competing architects could use the drawing to envision their own concepts and ideas to commemorate westward expansion.

Eero Saarinen, at age 38, was declared the winner of the JNEM competition in 1948. His daring design of a huge arch on the St. Louis riverfront brought him international attention and acclaim within the architectural community. Born in Finland in 1910, Eero Saarinen was the son of Eliel Saarinen, a noted and respected architect. His mother, Loja, was a gifted sculptor, weaver, photographer, and architectural model maker. The Saarinens emigrated to the United States in 1923 when Eliel was asked to become the first president of the Cranbrook Institute of Architecture and Design. Eero was schooled at Cranbrook, at the Yale School of Architecture, and in Europe. He spent most of his early career as a partner in his father's architectural firm, and was best known prior to winning the JNEM competition for his furniture designs.

THE ARCH BEGAN WITH PIPECLEANERS
Eero Saarinen,
St. Louis Post-Dispatch, March 7, 1948

So many people have asked us just how we arrived at the arch motif for the Jefferson National Expansion Memorial Competition that I thought I would try to trace back the thoughts that led us to this solution.

I remember once during the war when two other architects and myself strolled on the Mall in Washington and wondered what we might do as a solution were there to be an architectural competition for a great national monument.

I argued the case for the pure monument as opposed to the utilitarian. I felt that monuments like the Lincoln and Washington monuments served their real purpose in reminding us of the great past, which is so important in relation to looking toward the future. I can remember many other similar discussions after the war which related to war memorials.

When the Jefferson National Expansion Memorial Competition was announced and I began to search in my mind for some basic simple form that such a monument might take, I can remember thinking how, in Washington, the memorials to our three greatest men – Washington, Lincoln and Jefferson – each has a distinct geometric shape: The Washington Monument, a vertical line; the Lincoln Memorial, a cube; and the Jefferson Memorial, a globe. There is something simple and satisfying in that, and I wondered whether a monument in St. Louis to Jefferson and the westward expansion should not have a shape along lines of the monument to him in Washington.

We began to imagine some kind of a dome which was much more open than the Jefferson Memorial in Washington. Maybe it could be a great pierced concrete dome that touched the ground on just three points. Taking advantage

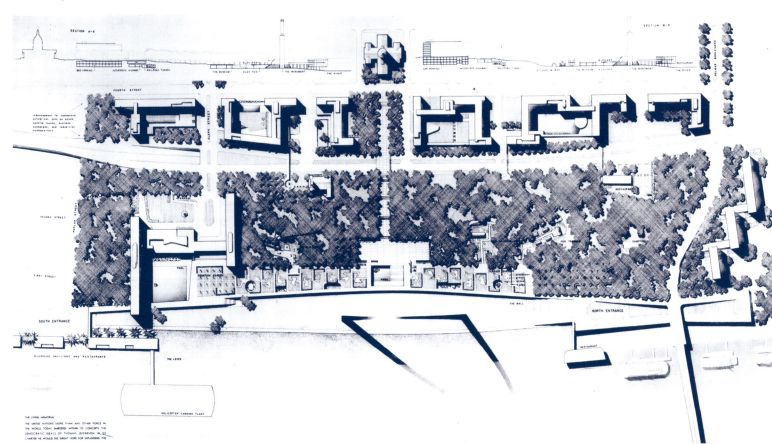

of modern methods of construction, something quite exciting could be done …

It was obvious that the memorial should be near the levee – but what kind of a memorial? In our minds we played with some great mass of stone pointing west. Then I remembered the thoughts of the previous session. Some great pierced dome? No, that seemed too heavy in relation to the long line of the levee. Then we tried the three ribs that came together and formed a kind of dome.

We tried it in a very crude way; the only things we could find to make it with were some pipe cleaners. But the three legs did not seem to fit in the plan, so we tried it with two legs, like a big arch.

We thought of a huge concrete arch. Such a shape was in no way unfamiliar to us. There are the dirigible hangars in Orly, France, designed by the engineer Freyssinet, that really gave a sense of monumentality. There are the arched concrete bridges that were built by the Swiss engineer, Maillart. There is also the arch that the great French architect, Le Corbusier, incorporated in his competition design for the Palace of the Soviets some time in the '20s. My father and myself had used some large exposed wooden arches to hold up the roof of the summer opera house we built at the Berkshire Music Center a few years ago.

All these things came to one's mind when we struggled to make an arch made of pipe cleaners stand upright on the plan on the living room rug. Then we thought maybe an arch is a good idea, but we began to wonder whether one leg should not be placed on each shore of the river, thus forming sort of a great symbolic arch bridge that tied together the

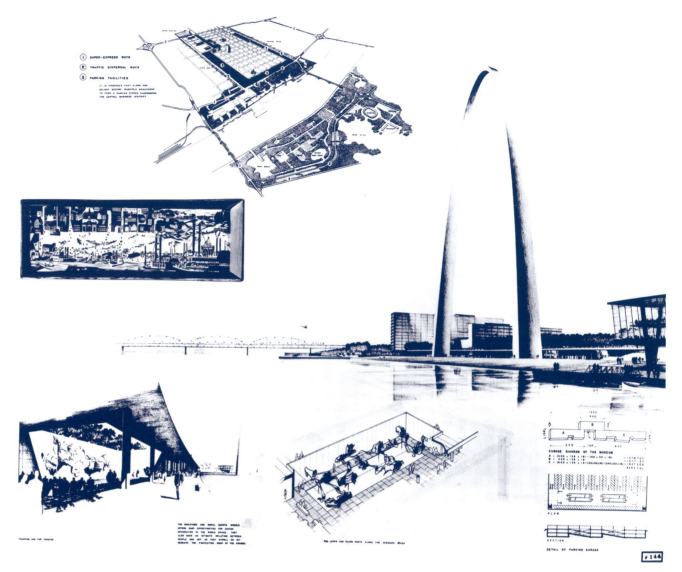

two sides of the Mississippi. No, there seemed to be enough bridges, and placing a symbolic bridge between two useful bridges didn't seem right. Maybe the arch should be parallel with the levee but placed right in the Mississippi. Then we came back to the thought that placing it on the west bank was not bad at all. It seemed like sort of a modern adaptation of a Roman triumphal arch …

More and more, it began to dawn on us that the arch was really a gateway, and various friends who stooped to look at what we were doing immediately interpreted it as such. Gradually, we named it the "Gateway to the West."

Details in this second entry board of 1947 from the Saarinen team include (clockwise, from top), an aerial rendering showing the memorial, the river, and plans for a future east side development; a view imagined from the river showing the Arch standing on the levee, with the museum building rising behind the south leg, the arcade running low behind the Arch, and the windowed river restaurant on the right; a plan and section for the proposed parking garage; a detail of the proposed sculpture garden along the arcade, with Lily Saarinen's sculpted animals of westward expansion; a view looking along the concrete-roofed arcade promenade, showing large murals; and a framed inset of a painting of the historic St. Louis riverfront.

27

DESIGNING A COMPETITION ENTRY
Dan Kiley,
Landscape Architect

I first met Eero in 1942. He was chief of the presentation branch of the O.S.S. doing visual and graphic studies for the conduct of the war, for the Joint Chiefs of Staff. We did a competition for a project in Ecuador, and we were among the five finalists.

I got this note from him in 1947, it was a little letter in mirror-writing, and it said, there's this big competition coming up, the first one after the war, and he said that it would be a wonderful chance to get established, and he asked me if I'd be interested in joining him. This was before he began working on the design; he'd just started to think about it. And I wrote back and said, "Yes, I'd love to." And I suggested he come to New Hampshire. We lived in a little house; we

couldn't put anybody up as guests, but my wife's rich cousin had a beautiful big house on the dirt road above us, so they could stay there. And so Eero and Lily came, and we talked. I had a little house on a dirt road, and opposite was a little barn. I had made a little office in the back of the barn, but upstairs it was just a loft with hay. When Eero came, he was tired, so he went up into the loft and took a 20-minute nap. And then he came down to work.

We talked in general about symbols. He liked to bounce things off me. He had the Arch idea already when he came there, as a symbol. He discussed with me his different symbolic approaches to the monument, and he came with a little sketch of the Arch. And then we talked about other symbols, and also how the 80-acre park would relate to the symbol.

(Opposite page, top) This photograph of Daniel Urban Kiley was submitted along with the 1947 Jefferson National Expansion Memorial competition entry. Eero Saarinen enjoyed a fruitful collaboration with Kiley on most of his designs between 1944 and Saarinen's death in 1961, resulting in the brilliant Kiley landscapes at Dulles Airport, the Miller House in Columbus, Indiana, and the John Deere Headquarters in Moline, Illinois.

These three watercolor perspective images were painted by Peter Ker Walker of the Office of Dan Kiley in 1962. They imagine the Arch landscape as proposed by Kiley in three seasons of the year, with tall rows of stately tulip poplar trees and the Arch in the background. The landscape, more than any other single component of the memorial design, continued to evolve between 1947 and 1964, when Kiley left the project.

What we tried to do on the site itself was to get a very simple forest, not a mixture of trees, we wanted to get a typical Midwestern landscape. I wanted the whole park to be one forest of one or two species; plus flowering trees and edge trees, like you see on a typical road when you go through the forest. You always have flowering trees that like the sun on the edges, and in the forest it's beautiful, it's like a cathedral. It has a sacred quality – like the columns in a church. And I was trying to seek that quality.

Eero was a very tough taskmaster. And the people who worked for him really had to be very dedicated to take it. One of the things I always remember is that Eero was just filled with the one thing called architecture. He thought of nothing else. He never listened to music, he had no activities. He was a fierce competitor, very fierce, even with his father. And he would go to every length to make sure that he was going to win.

We worked on it for a week in New Hampshire, then he went back to his offices in Bloomfield Hills, Michigan. During the second phase of the competition I lived with him for four months, worked every night, all night long, 'til three or four in the morning. We'd

usually get up at 9 or 9:30. That went on for four months. I worked doing the drawings, working on the contours.

In both the first and the second phases, I was trying to interject a more spatial mystery into the whole site. Not a kind of static, dry form; the landscape should relate more spatially, like a walk in nature. It should be like a walk in the woods, and you don't know what's coming next. And it's leading you, always leading you. I call it spatial continuity.

THE COMPETITION COMMENCES
Harry B. Richman,
Architect

WE were in our junior year in the Washington University School of Architecture in 1947-1948. One of our instructors asked Bob Israel and I if we would want to volunteer our services in helping the jury during their judging of the Jefferson National Expansion Memorial architectural competition. While the task would take about three days from our busy school schedule, the opportunity was too good to pass up.

Our first task was to uncrate and unwrap the 172 competition entries submitted by architects from across the United States. Each entry consisted of two presentation boards which measured 36" x 48" and represented the initial stage of a two-stage competition. We placed the boards on easels arranged in rows in two large rooms on the second floor of the Old Courthouse.

Bob and I divided the work. With each entry we unpacked, we could only guess the name of the architect (anonymity was a program requirement, and each entry only had a number) and play amateur jurors looking for the best design. As eager students of architecture, we discussed the merits of each of the best entries and could not resist rendering our judgments and ranking them. Of course, we speculated on what the jurors in their final deliberation would select as the finalists. I unscrewed the plywood panel from the crate containing the entry that was to become number 144, carefully removed the protective covering over the presentation boards, and gazed at Eero Saarinen's stunning concept for the memorial. I called Bob over to share my excitement. Were we looking at the winning entry?

We had unpacked many entries that day that were creative and beautifully presented. Saarinen's inspired solution, elegantly rendered, was a daring departure from other proposals that, while often competent, were limited to conventional architectural responses to the competition program. We were stirred by the Saarinen design and wondered whether the jurors would be up to the challenge of embracing the scale, audacity, and beauty of Saarinen's bold concept.

JEFFERSON NATIONAL EXPANSION MEMORIAL

(Top) In 1948 Bill Eng, born in Canton, China, was a graduate student at the University of Illinois at Champaign-Urbana, and had worked for Eliel Saarinen at Cranbrook. He went on to work for Louis Kahn and Eero Saarinen, and after 1960 to teach architecture at Champaign-Urbana until his death as an emeritus professor in 2005.

(Bottom) This second-round design of 1948, by William Eng, Gordon A. Phillips, and George N. Foster, won second prize in the JNEM competition. It was a complete reworking of the trio's 1947 submission, and included seven pylons on the left, each of which commemorated a historic event in the acquisition of the West, while large museum buildings on the right told the story. The judges noted its "breadth of treatment and an uncluttered quality, with excellent placing of individual elements," and applauded its connection to the city.

31

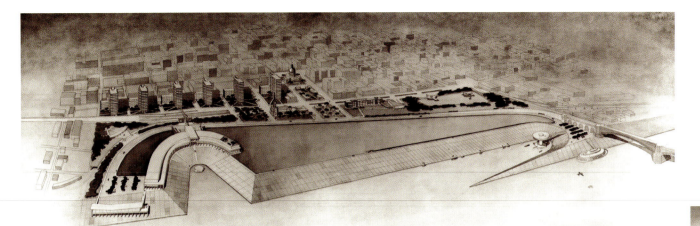

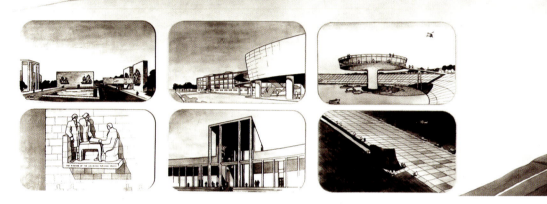

After the jurors did a preliminary walk-through on September 23, 1947, they gathered at the conference table to discuss the program and the criteria that would frame their deliberations. Among the criteria that would be adopted, I remember at least two: the levee must not be altered, and a bridge over the Mississippi would not be an acceptable memorial. Consequently, several fine entries, or so it seemed to us, were dropped from contention.

As the jurors continued their examination of the entries over the next three days, those that were rejected were removed from the easels and the preferred entries were moved forward. After several passes, the preferred entries were gradually narrowed to a select few. The objective of the jury was to designate five finalists. We were fascinated by the jury process, and observed with increasing anticipation that with each successive vote the Saarinen proposal stood out as the number one entry in the order of preference. The jurors did not disappoint!

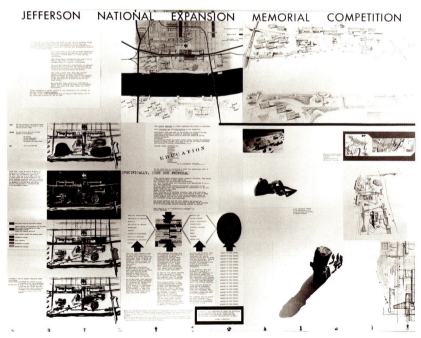

(Opposite page, top left) Design number 41 was submitted by Harris Armstrong of Kirkwood, Missouri. The perspective rendering and detail board, reproduced here, shows the audacity and daring innovation of his simple design, which dramatically altered the levee. The judges thought the design impractical and objected to the harsh nature of the proposal to a pedestrian actually walking in the space, for whom the sweeping curves, seen at ground level, would have no meaning.

(Opposite page, bottom left) This photograph of Harris Armstrong was included with his 1947 submission; he was chosen as one of two runners-up (fourth/fifth place) when the winner was announced in 1948. Armstrong was the only solo entrant among the five finalists.

(Opposite page, top right) Although the judges lambasted Harris Armstrong's 1947 proposal, they felt it showed promise, and Armstrong was chosen as one of the five semi-finalists. His resubmitted design of 1948 was a complete reworking of his original concept. This proposal included a large central structure of a rather featureless rectangular block, and a studied, formal landscape design.

(Opposite page, bottom right) This detail board was part of the 1947 submission of Charles and Ray Eames. Like many famous architects, the Eames' entry was eliminated in round one. Other round one rejections included Walter Gropius, Edward D. Stone, and Skidmore, Owings and Merrill.

(Top) The detail board from entry number 25 showed design elements of the plan submitted by Frank Weise, Brewster Adams and Gyo Obata, with paintings by Emerson Woelffer. Obata was later famous as a senior partner in the firm Hellmuth, Obata and Kassebaum.

(Bottom) This perspective view of Eliel Saarinen's entry, number 147, was rendered by J. Barr, and featured a gigantic rectangular memorial feature pierced by three portals facing north and south. The plan called for a large breakwater on the Mississippi, and extensive landscaping and harbor redesign on the east side. Eliel Saarinen was such a well-known architect in 1947 that the competition advisor, George Howe, jumped to the conclusion when seeing that a Saarinen had been chosen as one of the five finalists that it was Eliel, and sent a telegram informing him. It was only later that Howe realized that Eliel's son, Eero, had actually submitted entry 144. Eliel's entry was not one of the five finalists.

EERO SAARINEN AND ASSOCIATES
WIN FIRST PRIZE
Charles Nagle,
JNEM Architectural Competition
Jury Member, 1947-1948

THE award was made with little hesitation and complete unanimity, as it were. We had discussed all the different proposals, and when we had discussed them all the chairman of the jury, Mr. Wurster, said, "Shall we have a trial ballot?" As you know it is usually just something to see how things are going, a general trend, and we thought, sure, we were ready for a trial ballot, so we had a trial ballot and it was unanimous, so there was no sense in taking more ballots.

There were 172 submissions, from all over the country and from Mexico, Alaska and from Hawaii. Eero Saarinen was the winner, and his team included two other designers, a landscape architect, and his wife, who is a sculptor. For the competition they were supplied with very complete documents, engineering documents giving all the actual grades involved on the riverfront, perspective photographs, and all kinds of data they would need to produce drawings.

The thing that is most interesting to me about this plan is that it is such a very complete plan, it solves every problem that was posed to the competitors. There were a great many plans and a great many problems to solve. The routing of the traffic past the Old Courthouse and down Third Street, the railroad, "which could have taken any route at all across the area as long as it was below the present grade," and the problem of the existing buildings which had to be retained: the Old Courthouse, the Old Cathedral, and Manuel Lisa's Warehouse, which is underneath the Arch. And I think the solution to those problems was brilliant, because if you'll notice the Old Cathedral was given its own plaza with several old buildings reerected around it. And a special roadway was brought in leading up to the Cathedral. You have a parking area convenient to the Cathedral, a museum building, and a restaurant building. The Manuel Lisa Warehouse has been utilized as an entrance feature to the memorial, the great parabolic arch. And it is done with great respect. It is a very beautiful form, I believe, and also a very symbolic form in that it suggests the Gateway to the West. The elevator within the Arch will be entered from the old warehouse; on top of the Arch there will be an observation amphitheater. You notice how happily the arch of the memorial feature frames the Old Courthouse. They have used landscaping and trees to great effect.

A competition is a costly thing to hold, and I think this is one of the most generously financed competitions in recent years. It is fair to say, I think, that when you are considering a $30 million project, for the sum of $225,000 you get the very best ideas, and it was money well spent.

Mr. Saarinen is a very reserved young man but he was very delighted indeed. It was a very exciting occasion when the announcement of the award was made.

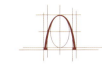

A Timeless Memorial
from a Master Architect
Susan Saarinen,
Landscape Architect, Daughter of Eero Saarinen

I was two years old when Dan Kiley and his wife came to live with us for four months. Both my father and grandfather had entered the Jefferson National Expansion Memorial Competition and were preparing separate submissions. My father Eero had grown up underneath my grandfather Eliel's drafting table, and now wanted to prove himself. The competitive spirit was fierce.

Following months of secrecy in an office divided down the middle by huge sheets of paper over the glass partitions, Dan and Eero worked until late hours almost every night preparing the final submission. Dan later told me that Eero would nightly announce that they needed to finish "just one more thing" before they went to bed. This usually meant that they would go to bed around three o'clock in the morning!

I'm not sure who first told me the story about the end of the competition. As I remember it, Eliel received a telegram congratulating him on being chosen as one of the five semi-finalists in the competition. The family broke out a bottle of champagne and toasted him. Two hours later the family received a phone call from an embarrassed competition official. A mistake had been made. It was, in fact, Eero who had advanced and had the chance to win the competition. Eliel, a very proud father, broke out a second bottle of champagne and everyone toasted my father.

I never actually saw my father searching for a style or an attitude with which to approach a particular project. All artists and designers do this, but it is an intensely personal process. From my perspective it seemed that my father drew loose sketches, sometimes on his calendar or another handy piece of paper, and had long and lively conversations with colleagues who were busily producing technical drawings. Suddenly models would appear. The models were essential. We had chains hanging in our basement so that he could study the proportions of a catenary curve. There was a huge, full-scale model of the stairs for the arch, so that he could be certain that changing treads on the stairs would be walkable. There was a tram car model at the office. Eero had everyone, including visitors, climb in and out, and he timed them with a stopwatch to estimate how many people the tram cars could carry in an hour.

In the latter half of the 19th century, a new architecture was inspired by the Industrial Revolution and the belief that good city planning and architecture would benefit society. In 1914, against the backdrop of the Arts and Crafts movement and Art Nouveau, Le Corbusier's Domino House created a new paradigm for architecture. It was during this time that Eero, the son of an extraordinarily talented architect, grew up in a family dedicated to the intellectual and practical exploration of design excellence. He approached each project with intense focus, dedication and discipline. When he finally turned to architecture, it was his fascination for geometry and his early studies in sculpture that would ultimately influence the forms his architecture would take.

(Left) On June 10, 1950, President Harry S Truman examined a model of the Jefferson National Expansion Memorial project during a visit to St. Louis. The others in the photo, from left to right, are Missouri Governor Forrest Smith, St. Louis Mayor Joseph M. Darst, President Truman, and Luther Ely Smith on the far right. Smith loved the idea of the Arch, and felt that it encapsulated perfectly the original concept he had in 1933 for a memorial to westward expansion.

(Right) On the evening of February 18, 1948, the winner of the JNEM competition was announced at a dinner given at the Statler Hotel in St. Louis. This photograph was taken as the check for $40,000 was given to the winning design team. Seen here are, from left to right, draftsman J. Barr, painter Alexander Girard, landscape architect Dan Kiley, sculptor Lillian Swan Saarinen, and architect Eero Saarinen. Competition judge William Wurster hands Eero the check.

It can be said of most architects that they have a certain recognizable style and materials preference that runs through most of their architecture. Eero's style is less easily described, as each project was approached as a unique opportunity to explore the spirit and expression of the building, the site, and new materials and technology.

In addition to his steady exploration of technologies and materials and his search for expression, three elements stand out in Eero's work: 1.) A large percentage is very sculptural, 2.) The delineation between walls and ceilings is blurred through his use of sculptural architecture, and 3.) Geometry plays a large part in many of his most memorable designs. My father did not live to see computer-aided design working for architecture, but his architecture ultimately may have contributed to a paradigm shift when computers became the daily tool of architects.

The Gateway Arch, as the memorial has come to be known, is arguably Eero Saarinen's greatest design. Dynamic and timeless, it fully embodies the pioneer spirit of the American people and has the power to inspire across all nations and cultures.

(Top) The plan and section for the Saarinen team's 1948 second round entry shows fewer revisions than the other four finalists made to their submissions. The team followed the advice of the jury and opened a vista in the forested landscape between the Arch and the Old Courthouse. The Arch, now triangular in cross section and a catenary rather than a parabolic curve, has been moved to be nearly on axis with the center line of the Courthouse dome.

(Bottom) J. Barr's imaginative and realistic rendering of the Gateway Arch as seen from the southwest gave the best vision to date of what the completed structure would look like. The view is surprising to modern observers because it looks so much like the completed memorial, yet was rendered in 1948. Note the international style restaurant buildings in the foreground, the late 1940s autos, the heavily forested grounds, and the fact that the Arch is placed on the levee.

CHAPTER 3

DESIGNED TO LAST A THOUSAND YEARS

1958-1962

*A*fter the excitement of the memorial competition, a lack of federal funds threw the Jefferson National Expansion Memorial back into limbo in 1948. Eero Saarinen turned to other projects, many of them brilliantly realized designs such as the chapel at the Massachusetts Institute of Technology, the U.S. Chancellery Buildings at Oslo, Norway and London, England, the David S. Ingalls Hockey Rink at Yale University, the TWA Terminal at John F. Kennedy International Airport, the John Deere and Company Headquarters in Moline, Illinois, the Dulles International Airport Terminal Building in Chantilly, Virginia, and the CBS Headquarters Building in New York City.

There were two major obstacles to the memorial becoming a reality. The first was what to do about the unsightly elevated railroad tracks along the riverfront in the memorial area. The second was finding funds to build it. Nearly everyone agreed that the railroad tracks should be moved, but no one could decide how to do this, or who should pay for it. The argument

continued until 1957, when it was solved by St. Louis Mayor Raymond R. Tucker. Mayor Tucker was a trained engineer, and designed a series of tunnels and cuts through which the railroad could pass in front of the Arch, a solution the railroads themselves, the National Park Service, and Eero Saarinen could all agree on. But running the railroad between the Arch and the river forced a redesign of the project by Eero Saarinen beginning in 1957. The primary features of the Arch, the tree-lined mall, and river overlooks were retained, but the surface structures of the original plan were placed underground, and a completely revamped landscape plan was developed by Saarinen and Dan Kiley. The system of curving, tree-lined walks they designed reflected the shape of the Arch. In fact, the entire landscape of the grounds was a vital part of the overall artistic design.

The other major problem, money, was solved when a balanced federal budget released funds for the memorial's construction in 1958. During the next three years Saarinen decided on the ultimate height of the Arch, 630 feet, and the exact type of weighted catenary curve which would be used. The Arch was designed to be beautiful from all angles, as seen from below and from various distances. It was, in reality, a piece of outdoor sculpture.

(Opposite Page) This photograph of the north floodwall and completed Gateway Arch shows off the spectacular nature of the memorial. The Arch was designed as a catenary curve. Derived from the Latin word for chain, "catenary" is defined as the shape assumed by a chain when its ends hang freely from two separated points. This shape was inverted to create the Arch.

(Left) Raymond R. Tucker was mayor of St. Louis from 1952 to 1964. Tucker attended St. Louis University and Washington University, and later headed the engineering department at Washington University. Tucker chaired the committee which cleaned up smoke pollution in St. Louis, and also was an outspoken champion of integration in the city. Tucker aggressively supported the Arch project and used his engineering background to untangle the thorny problem of the railroad trestle along the levee.

(Right) This photo shows the old railroad trestle prior to being dismantled, with the new series of tunnels and open railroad cuts under construction next to it in the upper right corner. Construction on this phase of the project took place in 1959 and 1960.

THE ARCH AS AN ARCHITECTURAL MASTERPIECE
Eugene Mackey,
FAIA, Architect, Mackey and Mitchell Associates

IN his creation of the Gateway Arch, Eero Saarinen's design process was seamless, perfectly marrying purpose, meaning, form, material and technology. He was energetically focused, obsessing not just on how something looked, but on how it was made. In creating a great memorial of our time, yet for all time, he selected form, function, meaning and process as one. In doing so, he infused the design with intellectual power and strength.

Saarinen and Fred Severud, his structural engineer, began by developing many design sketches and drawings. These dealt with design and the process of construction, and therefore, how the details could be resolved. One of their best decisions was to employ a stainless steel stressed skin, found primarily on airplanes, as the finish material. They also speculated on extending elevator technology for internal vertical circulation and selected creeper crane strategies as the method for each leg to grow skyward.

For Eero Saarinen, each project was an opportunity to seek true meaning, explore the most fundamental assumptions, and pursue new answers within the context of advanced technology. Each job was a blank sheet of paper where he could focus his immense talent. Saarinen was not one to be limited by a movement or style; he solved problems on their own terms in the context of a rigorous, disciplined methodology. You can understand why each of his designs is so singularly unusual. Just think of the contrast between the TWA Terminal, John Deere's corporate headquarters, collegiate housing at Yale, and the Jefferson National Expansion Memorial. Each of these projects was unique, but what they have in common is: (1) an inspired idea, (2) exploration of just the right expression, and (3) unusual application of materials. As an architect, Saarinen was always challenging, demanding, and never satisfied until it was right in his mind.

Many years ago, there was a design conference in Aspen, Colorado, which attracted all the major architects of Saarinen's generation. Each was given a white 12" x 12" square, and a series of colored 1" x 1" squares. Twenty minutes later they turned them in. Philip Johnson, full of himself as usual, sought out Saarinen to proclaim that he had produced a design only using the black and white squares. Saarinen slyly responded, "Well, I only used the white one."

With the benefit of time, the Arch is truly as fresh a concept as the day he conceived it. In that regard, Saarinen's Gateway Arch has transcended the Modern Movement. Within the region, the Arch marks the Mississippi River from afar. Its dynamic form evolves like a hibiscus bloom, opening and closing from centenary curve to obelisk as you move around it. It magically reflects the sun and sky, changing color continuously along its triangular profile, seamless with its scale and strength. The Gateway Arch at the Jefferson National Expansion Memorial is without question the greatest modern memorial of the 20th century and symbolizes the great American it honors.

The color, drama, and sculptural qualities of Eero Saarinen's work can be seen in his designs for the TWA Terminal in New York City (built 1956-1962, top) and Dulles International Airport Terminal outside Washington, D.C. (1958-1962, bottom). With TWA he ambitiously developed a gigantic concrete shell in a sculptural form suggestive of the act of flight. The soaring quality of the interiors also puts passengers in the mood for the adventure of their journey.

Saarinen studied the mechanics of flight and the circulation of passengers within existing terminals prior to designing Dulles, the first terminal specifically crafted for large jet aircraft. Saarinen sought to eliminate the long distances people were forced to walk because of the size of each jetway, gate and pad, and so devised a shuttle system to take passengers to their planes. His design also allowed for the expansion of the soaring, glass-walled main terminal without spoiling the plan by prescribing the extension of each end using the same slanted columns and concave roofline; this expansion was conducted in the 1990s. Saarinen personally planned every aspect of most of his structures, down to the smallest detail; in the case of Dulles, he even prescribed the font to be used on all the signs in the building.

DESIGNING THE GATEWAY ARCH
Kevin Roche,
Architect, Roche-Dinkeloo

WHEN Eero Saarinen won the competition for the Jefferson National Expansion Memorial in 1948, everyone in the architectural world was aware of his design as well as the confusion which resulted from the assumption that his father, Eliel, had won. There was great excitement and great expectation that the project would proceed. However, when I joined Eero's office in the spring of 1951, the project seemed to be almost forgotten. It appeared to have been lost in the maze of Washington, and even in our small office of about 10 to 12 people it was rarely discussed at that time. Eero was preoccupied with other large projects, notably the General Motors Technical Center and various other works at university campuses such as Brandeis, Michigan, MIT, and Yale.

It was not until 1958, when it was resurrected, that Eero was able to focus on it again. He identified five areas of study: the development of the levee, overlooks, railroad passage, and stairs; the development of the Arch itself; the exploration of the mechanics of getting visitors to the top of the Arch; the design of the museum and the method of telling the story of the Louisiana Purchase, the Lewis and Clark expedition and the opening of the West; and, finally, the overall landscape design and its relationship to the courthouse and the city. It was characteristic of Eero that in every one of these areas of study

and design he explored innumerable possibilities involving many detailed models as well as many, many sketches and renderings.

When the steps which compose the great sweep up from the river to the Arch were under study, there was concern that their variable width could be a hazard to people traversing them. Consequently, a large, full-size mockup was built to test the safety as well as the visual impact that the steps would have. National Park Service Director Conrad Wirth and Superintendent George Hartzog were invited to visit the office in Bloomfield Hills to see this mock up, which they did; and they were suitably impressed. Eero took the opportunity at that same meeting to discuss the theme of the museum and how it could be developed and presented. He was eager to have his old friend Charles Eames undertake this aspect of the project, so he asked Charles to send him some recent works. Charles sent a 16 mm copy of a program that he had just completed for CBS on the Fifties. I set up the projector in the conference room, and we started this film, which featured Ethel Merman, among others, and terminated with Ethel singing at the top of her voice, "Everything's Coming up Roses." If you have ever heard Ethel Merman deliver this song, it is a pretty numbing experience. I had neglected to turn down the volume, so Director Wirth got it full blast. When the film finished there ensued a deep silence which seemed to last for many minutes and was eventually broken by Director Wirth saying, in a very dry voice, "Was there anything else you wished to discuss?" So ended the possibility that Charles would be involved with the project.

In designing the Arch, many studies were made to determine the proper curvature, and while the curve was that of a catenary such as would be formed by a chain hung upside down, the development included studying the impact of a weighted catenary which would slightly modify the simple catenary form. Again – many models, studies, section drawings, many chains hung from the ceiling with weights.

The structural design of the Arch was developed by Fred Severud, a brilliant engineer, aided by a young German engineer who was his associate, Hannskarl Bandel. The concept of the steel shell filled with concrete for the initial one-third of the structure, and from there on built without concrete, was the result of Severud working with Eero and a team including John Dinkeloo, Eero's partner. At the same time a proposal developed to use carbon steel clad with stainless steel. Several large plates of stainless steel-clad carbon steel were delivered to the office for study from both engineering and aesthetic points of view.

The mechanics of getting visitors to the top of the Arch was beginning to evolve when Eero heard about Richard Bowser, who had considerable experience inventing automatic systems for moving cars in multi-floor garages. There were many meetings with Dick, who came up with the idea of the capsule which could rotate as it traveled from the underground station up the leg of the Arch to the visitors' platform at the top. We constructed many models of the underground station and built a full-size model of the five-person capsule to test with passengers of various sizes. We also built a full-size cross section through the top of the Arch so that the viewing windows could be small enough to not be visible from the outside but large enough to provide the visitor with a spectacular view. Much effort went into this model to ensure that children and adults of all heights could reach the viewing windows comfortably.

Eero felt that the landscaping was a key element of the design and, with J. Henderson Barr, made many studies back and forth with Dan Kiley. The final form of the landscaping and the sweeping approach of trees to the Arch from the courthouse was Eero's, developed by Dan.

After Eero's untimely death, the project was carried forward by the team in the Saarinen office who had worked on it through the various stages of development, in particular John Dinkeloo and Joe Jensen (who subsequently joined the Park Service).

The great tragedy, of course, is that Eero died before the work on the site was completed and before the structure of the Arch itself was started. Eero would surely have appreciated seeing the Arch in all of its splendor and particularly would have enjoyed riding to the top and experiencing firsthand the visitor's excitement and awe of this marvelous structure which celebrates an extraordinary moment in American history.

Between 1947 and his death in 1961, Eero Saarinen, pictured here with some of his many Arch models, lavished years of intense labor and thought on the design, perfecting his vision with constant changes and improvements. The precise shape of the curve, the amount of taper between the base and the top, the exact nature of the landscape design, and many other elements occupied his office between 1958 and 1961.

PLANNING A MUSEUM
Bill Everhart, Historian,
JNEM, 1959-1962; Assistant Director for
Interpretation, NPS, 1964-1970;
Director, Harpers Ferry Center, 1970-1975

An early incarnation of the museum design is shown in this cutaway view, which also shows the operation of the tram cars. The concept includes a series of room-like exhibit spaces, an idea later avoided by museum designer Aram Mardirosian. Mardirosian felt that visitors to the museum should be able to see the exit at all times, so that they would be able to get to their tram ride or a movie shown within the visitor center complex on time.

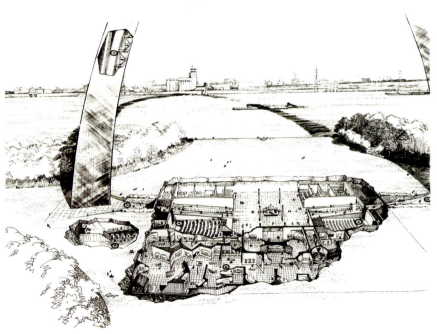

I joined the staff of Jefferson National Expansion Memorial because George Hartzog, the superintendent, would not take no for an answer. He called from St. Louis one day late in 1959, offering me a job. I already had a rewarding assignment, identifying historic sites of national significance in the West, with duty station in that noble city, San Francisco. George asked me, without preliminaries, "How would you like to take charge of planning the largest museum in the National Park System?"

He urged a prompt decision, warning that if I stayed in San Francisco I'd lose my edge "like the rest of the lotus eaters in that regional office." I told him I'd think it over, giving me time for a few phone calls to friends who knew or had worked for George. All rated him highly: "a bias for bold action"; "a low threshold for underachievers"; "stuck permanently in overdrive." Of course I took the job.

At St. Louis I recruited a staff of historians equally adept at research and interpretation, a term the Park Service prefers over education. The chief aim of interpretation is not instruction but provocation, whether conducting a nature walk, producing a film, or designing museum exhibits.

Staff historians were assigned to the various frontiers, such as mining or the Rocky Mountain fur trade, highlighting pivotal events and individuals who played significant roles. An exhibit designer attached to the history team would sketch exhibit ideas. Some seemed doable, others not, including one in particular that stated the case brilliantly. "How could we convey the scene in the White House when Thomas Jefferson unrolled the maps of the known West and said to his private secretary, Meriwether Lewis, 'This is what I want you to do.'"

When the National Park Service's Mission 66 program began in 1956, there was very little construction money, and in the ten-year life of Mission 66 something like 120 visitor centers were built. So the museum branch had the problem of going from having plenty of time to do one museum every couple of years, to doing six, eight, maybe even ten a year. And the way they did that, which is understandable if not forgivable, was they developed a system which we called "museum minestrone" in which they had so many panels per museum, and so many cases, and one diorama always. Well, all of

the museums looked alike, they had a formula. George and I thought we've got to do better than that. So we decided to hire Eero Saarinen to do the museum. He would be the architect, he would be the major contractor to design the museum, and then he would hire other people. Eero liked the idea immensely. But the problem was to convince Director Connie Wirth to take the job away from the Park Service.

We took Eero on a tour of Park Service museums; he said that a National Park was "a place where you travel 1,000 miles to see a rusty nail in a glass case!" Eero got noted architect and designer Charles Eames involved, and also Broadway set designer Jo Mielziner. Of course Connie Wirth rejected Eames after seeing "The Fabulous Fifties" film, saying that the Park Service already had the best exhibit designers in the country, and this museum was going to be designed by the Park Service. So as a result of that, Saarinen was out. But, as it turned out, it didn't make a difference, because of

financial constraints. After two years of work, we had just finished the museum prospectus when the bids for construction of the Gateway Arch were opened. The lowest bid totally exhausted the ceiling set by Congress for the entire memorial.

Nearly a decade later, when George Hartzog was the director of the National Park Service, he was able to obtain funding for the design of the Museum of Westward Expansion. The contract was awarded to an architectural firm headed by Aram Mardirosian, a fine architect who had worked for the Saarinen design team. He produced a museum worthy of its place beneath the Gateway Arch – a museum that would ultimately fan out chronologically from a central bronze statue of Thomas Jefferson. How fitting that the person for whom the Memorial was named, the person who designed the Gateway Arch, and the person who designed the Museum of Westward Expansion, were all architects.

(Top right) As the erection of the Gateway Arch was ready to begin in early 1963, the visitor center and museum were covered by a roof with a waterproof membrane, seen as a white trapezoid in the upper central portion of this photo.

(Bottom) The underground museum is seen here under construction, showing two columns in the foreground with wooden forms on their exterior, waiting for the concrete to set.

(Top left) When first completed, the visitor center was a sterile, concrete room with a uniform grid of columns. The area reserved for the museum was similar, except that it had a dirt floor rather than terrazzo.

ENGINEERING THE ARCH
Fred Severud, Jr.,
Engineer, Son of the Engineer for the Arch Project

MY father, Fred Severud, was the founder of the firm now known as Severud Associates, a structural engineering company in New York City. He was a well-known innovator, having designed the first cable-supported roof structures in the U.S., including the Raleigh Coliseum, Madison Square Garden, and the Yale Hockey Rink (with the Saarinen firm), among others.

Besides the Yale Hockey Rink, he was the structural consultant on many other Saarinen projects. Probably his best-known project was the Gateway Arch in St. Louis. Although Eero Saarinen designed the look of the Arch, it was my father and his firm that worked out the way in which it could be built. Without the mathematical calculations worked out by the Severud firm, and the use of orthotropic engineering principles (meaning that the steel inner and outer walls of the Arch are the actual structural members, rather than a skeleton of girders with the steel panels hanging on them), there would be no Arch today. After many years of consultations and hard work, construction was finally begun in 1963.

The Arch was built as two cantilever structures, which eventually met at the top. The design had to consider the loadings and structural action at the various stages, while keeping in mind the practicalities of construction. During the initial cantilever stage, post-tensioned concrete was placed between the inner and outer skins, up to the 300-foot level, to provide the necessary strength for the inward curve of the legs. Above 300 feet the post-tensioned concrete was omitted. The structure was much too tall to build using conventional cranes, so in conjunction with the contractors, a climbing crane, which rode on rails attached to the outside, was used on each leg. At the 530-foot level, a temporary horizontal strut truss was placed from leg to leg, which then made the legs act together, an entirely different stress condition. Since the setting of the final piece was to be done during warm weather, a problem arose; the legs had different exposures to the sun, which caused them to be several feet different in elevation during the day, so all measurements were made at night, when there was no temperature difference. The construction team planned to also place the piece at night, when both sides would line up. When the mayor of

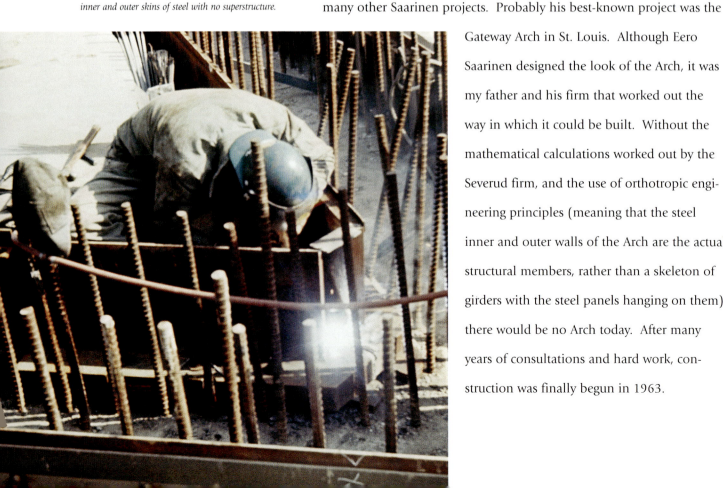

(Top) In this photograph taken in the mid-1940s, Fred Severud (left) can be seen gathered around a drafting table along with the other principals of his engineering firm, Messrs. Krueger, Bergen and Elstad. Without the crucial contributions of the Severud firm, the Arch could not have been engineered and constructed in its final completed form.

(Bottom) A workman welds part of the inner steel wall early in the construction process. The orthotropic construction designed by the Severud firm involved inner and outer skins of steel with no superstructure.

St. Louis heard of this plan, however, he stated that this was totally unacceptable. This was to be one of the most significant happenings in St. Louis history; the setting must be done during the early afternoon! This would cause a difference in elevation which couldn't be overcome; what could be done? My father woke up with the solution during the night: use water to cool down the hot side! The Fire Chief was contacted, and agreed to provide hoses and pumpers to spray the hot side. The result? The final piece was placed during the day, with no problem.

My father's outstanding quality as a structural engineer was that he really understood how structures work, on the deepest level.

From the start of his career, he made his reputation by solving the reasons for observed failures. He analyzed natural structures and forces, and applied their principles to man-made structures. He was one of the first structural engineers to analyze the forces from atomic blasts, and wrote an early textbook on protection from nuclear explosions called "The Bomb, Survival & You."

Even before my father retired in 1973, he combined his engineering knowledge with his ministry, becoming a dedicated teacher of engineering and the Bible. He was invited as a guest lecturer to many colleges & universities, to speak to architectural & engineering students about working with the principles of engineering (including those observable in nature) to make successful structures.

Above all else, he was a kind man. Even though he was exceptionally intelligent and talented, he never "talked down" to others. He treated all as equals, and as a result, he had everyone's deep respect. He inspired others to do their best by example and leadership. He was a humble man; in all the time I knew him, I don't recall ever seeing him lose his temper. When anyone caused him problems (as happens to everyone occasionally), he could always find some excuse for the other person, and find a way to work things out. He tried to pass on to his children a love for honesty and justice – he really believed in doing the right thing, even when it wasn't to his advantage. He applied his deep religious convictions in every aspect of his life; he lived his faith, didn't just preach it to others.

A creeper derrick was attached to each leg of the Arch in the first few months of construction. These derricks were raised periodically as the Arch increased in height.

BUILDING AN ARCH
Bruce Detmers,
Architect, Eero Saarinen and Associates

I joined the architectural firm of Eero Saarinen and Associates in June of 1956. When funds were made available in the late fifties I was assigned to the Jefferson Memorial project and was involved until the completion of the Arch in the late 1960s. Eero had just completed an addition to his office on Long Lake Road in Bloomfield, Michigan. My drafting board was located in the new part of the office in which the model of the Jefferson Memorial was located. The office was having meetings with members of the National Park Service at that period. Just outside of my window, Eero built a full-size model two stories high of the grand center stairs to demonstrate to the Park Service the scale of the steps.

I recall my first official visit to the site in St. Louis. The site was littered with piles of rubble, the remains of demolished buildings, old streets, and the elevated railroad trestle at the levee of the Mississippi River. The Old Cathedral stood alone at the edge of the site and appeared cut off from the city by the wide road on one side and the rubble on the other. The Old Courthouse, in which the historic Dred Scott trial occurred, looked dirty and gray. In my subsequent visits to St. Louis over the years, I attended countless meetings in this courthouse. Little did I realize on my first visit how much time I would be away from my family during my involvement in this project. My

third child was born while on a St. Louis trip with John Dinkeloo, the father of several children himself, who assured me that the baby would not be born on time.

Construction funds for the memorial became available in small amounts rather than a large bulk of money at one time. The first contract included realignment of the existing railroad tracks and construction of the street on the levee. The second contract included the flood protection walls, the North and South Overlook buildings at either end of the site, and the relocation of the elevated railroad tracks through tunnels and landscaped areas within the park. Eero said the high walls of the North and South Overlook buildings defined the extent of the site, like a period at the end of a sentence.

The improvements to the levee and relocation of the existing railroad tracks proved a challenging effort; however, the final design of the Arch lay ahead of us. Shaping the Arch was a trial and error process for Eero Saarinen. It was a challenging task to define dimensions of the sculptural shape. Accurate dimensions were necessary to make the construction a reality. Eero designed exclusively with models – there was no exception in the design of the Arch. Several models were made ranging in size from a few inches in height for placement on the site, to a scale model eight feet in height for detailed study of the Arch itself. Half models of the Arch were placed against a mirror, the reflection giving a sense of the full Arch. The height of the Arch was increased to 630 feet from 590 feet during this process.

The attempt to arrive at a curve for the Arch included suspending a rope fastened at its endpoints; the sagging rope formed a catenary curve, sort of an upside down arch. The adding of weights along the length of the suspended rope changed the shape of the curve. A uniform rope resulted in a curve that was too flat on top. The attempts to weight the suspended rope were not helpful in arriving at a shape to satisfy Eero.

The breakthrough came when Dr. Hannskarl Bandel, the project structural engineer with the firm of Severud, Elstad and Krueger Associates, provided us with weighted catenary formulas with which we could change the shape of the Arch by mathematical means. Numerical adjustments were made in the formula and plotted. The plotting process and that of making study models resulted in the final design of the Arch. The legs of the Arch are steeper and larger at the base; the top of the Arch smaller and less flat than a pure uniformly weighted centenary, resulting in the fact that the Arch seems to soar.

The final step in defining the Arch for construction was to use a formula to dimension the Arch. The formula was complex, taking many hours to calculate the hundreds of dimensions required to define the final form of the Arch. Our accounting department's mechanically operated machine could multiply tracking numbers to several decimal places. This (by today's standards) ancient technology was used to calculate the dimensions of the Arch. I was much relieved to learn that Pittsburgh Des Moines Steel, the subcontractor to fabricate the Arch structure, used a computer to check our calculations and found no errors.

(Top) Work continued on the relocation of the railroad tracks in 1960. This view shows the completed concrete retaining walls constructed on each side of the tracks. The solution worked out by Mayor Tucker ended a decade of wrangling with the question of what to do about the railroad right of way in front of the Arch.

(Middle) The completed railroad tracks enter a tunnel, which for reasons of fulfilling the compromise with railroad unions and the Terminal Railroad Association was always referred to as a "bridge."

(Bottom) The enormous flood wall rises high above Wharf Street and the St. Louis levee on the north end of the Arch grounds. At Eero Saarinen's insistence, the walls were built with the same catenary curve as the Arch itself, this time inverted. The effectiveness of the flood walls and their associated gates at the north and south ends of the grounds was successfully tested during the great flood of 1993.

"Give Us a Concept in Two Weeks"
Dick Bowser,
Designer of the Arch Tram System

In 1960 I stopped at the Montgomery Elevator Company in Moline, Illinois to see a friend of mine. I walked in, and he took a look at me, and he said something like "Holy Cow, why didn't I think about you?" I had no idea what he was referring to. He told his secretary to call somebody back. There was a very short telephone conversation introducing me to one of Eero Saarinen's partners. When we started talking to each other, their first questions were, "did elevators have to go vertically?" And I told them I didn't think so, because I'd seen my father make a special dumbwaiter that traveled sideways. The next question was, "When could I meet with Eero Saarinen?" I started hemming and hawing around; I wasn't looking for that kind of a job. I couldn't imagine somebody would even consider me for such a task. An individual like myself, with no organization and no college degree, in my own mind stood no chance for a design contract.

After meeting with Mr. Saarinen in Michigan he wanted to know if I could put some kind of a concept together for elevators in the Arch. There were some pretty high figures on daily visitation that they wanted to achieve, and I said, "Well, I'll try." They said we want to have you make a 45-minute presentation, and we'd like to have this in two weeks.

I went down to my basement and on my drawing board I started trying to figure out how to transport visitors to the top of the Arch. It

soon became apparent that nobody was going to put a square box of any size up through the triangular Arch legs. You wouldn't be able to carry anything. At the bottom of the Arch, you could use a large elevator, but up at the top you couldn't get a small elevator through the space. In fact, it was so restricted, escalators couldn't be used either; everything was at the wrong angles for escalators. So I reached a point where I was pretty discouraged. I thought I was pretty smart on elevators, but to try to do it in that triangularly-shaped space that was not plumb got to be quite a problem. I thought about Ferris wheel seats on chains, and running them all the way around, but there would have to be about a quarter of a mile of some real heavy chain. Things were just getting all out of proportion. So that's when I stopped.

First of all, I thought, the priority was that the elevator had to be able to fit into the top of the Arch, not the bottom. The bottom had lots of room. And then I thought surely they would like to have an emergency

Dick Bowser, inventor of the Arch tram system, was photographed with Arch memorabilia as part of a news story in the early 1990s. Dick's inventive solution to the problem of getting people to the top of the Arch amazed many architects and engineers who worked on the project, who shied away from attempting such a necessarily complicated design. Dick also worked with Eero Saarinen on a couple of other projects, including the mechanics of the mobile lounges for Dulles International Airport.

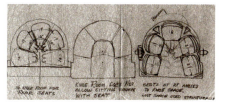

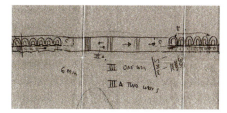

(Left) On October 21, 1965, a prototype tram capsule was examined by (left to right) Edwin B. Meissner, Jr., President of the St. Louis Car Company, which built the capsules; Robert C. Staudt of Planet Corporation, Lansing Michigan, responsible for the construction and installation of the tram system; and Col. R.E. Smyser, Jr., Director of Bi-State Development Agency. Lacking the funds to build the tram system, the National Park Service responded favorably to a request by Bi-State (today renamed Metro) to construct and operate it. The completed tram system efficiently takes visitors to the top of the Arch in four minutes. The same system designed by Dick Bowser, with minor modifications, has been in continuous use for over 35 years, and is still run by Metro.

(Right) Sketches of the interior of a capsule (to work out the seating arrangement) and of the unloading points near the top of the Arch hint at a collaboration between Dick Bowser and Eero Saarinen on the fine details of the tram system. It is thought that both men contributed to these drawings.

stairway up there, besides any equipment, for maintenance or emergencies. So then I started thinking, what can be done in half of the cross-section of the Arch at the top? Then I thought about the Ferris wheel seats again. People would have to be protected while traveling, so the seats would have to be enclosed. This was more and more looking something like a cement mixer barrel. I put seats into each barrel. A train of these barrels could provide the passenger-carrying capacities that they'd like to have. The more I thought about it, there was no reason why this couldn't be driven by an elevator machine; a standard elevator machine, with the cables and everything, and they could be made to meet the elevator code, and every safety feature in an elevator. And by the way, elevators have an excellent safety record, better than any other mode of public transportation.

51

This photograph shows tram capsules during the installation process. Shown at the top of the Arch, the capsules were later obscured by a wall and cosmetic decoration to create a more aesthetically pleasing debarkation point for visitors. Today, a series of small doors in the wall allows access and egress from the tram cars.

(Opposite page) As the concrete was formed for the foundation of the Arch legs and the visitor center, two "load zones" were also built according to Dick Bowser's specifications below ground level. In this view, at the lower center of the shot, can be seen the small doors which would later become the entrances to the tram ride. One of the toughest decisions made by Bowser was to tell the contractors how large a hole they should form in the base of the concrete foundations; too large and the foundation would be too weak, too small and the tram could not pass through. After much pondering, a rectangular hole of just the right size was left for the tram tracks and machinery.

My two weeks were up, and I traveled to Michigan to make the presentation in Saarinen's office. I was so naive, I thought I was going there just to talk to the architect. But when I got there, there were all kinds of consulting engineers, landscape architects, air conditioning experts, governors, senators, and congressmen, and the mayor of St. Louis, who fortunately was Raymond R. Tucker, who was an engineer. When I found this out, I thought at least there's one guy in the room that's going to know what I'm talking about. Being scheduled as the last presentation of the meeting, I had all day to sit there and worry. I had my notes, and you would laugh if you could have seen them. They were longhand notes with freehand sketches. Then it was my turn. There was a great deal of attention to my whole presentation. When I finished, there were a couple of hours of questions. Almost all of it was positive. I could detect a little heckling in a few places, and some questioning of my abilities. Inside, I've always carried a regret that I didn't have a college degree. And I remember right towards the end of this discussion, one man got up and I knew just from the way he asked the question, he wanted to know how much education I had. His question was: "Mr. Bowser, what are you?" And something told me, don't get in an argument with this man, so I just told him I was 38 years old, and everybody laughed, and that was the end of my credentials as far as being able to do the Arch. I still laugh about that, and I think it's the most appropriate answer I could have given. I was quite pleased. When the meeting was over, and we were getting ready to go to a restaurant, one of Saarinen's partners came over and said, "We're not going to have any trouble getting you a contract to do that." And I thought, "What have I done?!!" because it seemed like a mixed blessing.

CHAPTER 4
REACHING FOR THE SKY
1959-1963

By 1959 the memorial was ready to get underway. It had been 20 years since demolition began on the riverfront buildings. To most St. Louisans, the riverfront area was known as a municipal parking lot, and nothing more. MacDonald Construction Company of St. Louis was awarded the contract to relocate the railroad tracks, and on June 23, 1959 groundbreaking ceremonies shifted the project into high gear. The National Park Service brought in George B. Hartzog, Jr. as superintendent, who pushed the project through on local and national levels. Representatives Clarence Cannon and Leonor Sullivan, along with Senator Stuart Symington, made sure that federal funds were available. Eero Saarinen prepared working drawings and preliminary designs for the Arch and the visitor center to be located beneath it. Tragically, he died of a brain tumor in 1961, two years before construction of the Arch began, at the age of 51. It was left to others who shared Saarinen's vision to make the Arch a reality.

In March 1962, MacDonald Construction Company, having completed the railroad tunnels, river overlooks and floodwalls, was awarded the contract for building the Arch, in the amount of $11,442,418. At the contract signing it was announced that there wasn't enough money to build the proposed elevator train system to transport visitors to the top of the Arch. It was then that the Bi-State Development Agency, now known as Metro (established by the Missouri and Illinois state legislatures to promote the planning and development of transportation for the area in and around St. Louis) stepped into the picture. They generously offered to issue revenue bonds to provide funds to install the transportation system in the Arch and to operate it when the Arch was completed. The tram system would cost another $2,000,000. The first concrete was poured for the foundations of the Gateway Arch on June 27, 1962. On February 12, 1963, the first stainless steel section of the Arch was set into place.

(Opposite page) This aerial photograph shows the cleared site of the Arch ready for construction to begin.

(Top left) At 10:30 a.m. on Tuesday, June 23, 1959, as local business and civic leaders looked on, Mayor Raymond Tucker turned the first spade full of dirt, beginning the site construction in preparation for the Arch. National Park Service Director Conrad Wirth attended, and former Mayor Bernard Dickmann presented remarks during the ceremony.

(Top right) The northern portion of the grounds of the Arch had been used for many years as a parking lot for downtown workers and businesses.

(Bottom) Vice President Richard Nixon studies a model of the memorial with general contractor Gene MacDonald and former Mayor Bernard Dickmann, in the rotunda of the Old Courthouse.

(Top left) Robert "Gene" MacDonald was president of MacDonald Construction Company, the general contractor on the railroad relocation, floodwall, and Gateway Arch projects.

(Bottom) Ralph Aberle, Superintendent for MacDonald Construction Company, oversaw work during the entire JNEM project. Here he shakes hands with his boss, Gene MacDonald, on the day the Arch was completed in 1965.

(Top right and opposite page) A series of photographs shows some of the variety of tasks overseen by the MacDonald firm during the construction of the Gateway Arch from 1963 to 1966. As the general contractor, MacDonald was responsible for awarding the subcontracts, some of which went to companies like Southwest Ornamental Iron of Kansas City and Sachs Electric of St. Louis, which had worked for many years with MacDonald on building missile silos in Alaska. Pittsburgh-Des Moines Steel was by far the largest of the subcontractors, responsible for erecting the Arch structure itself.

Contracting for an Arch
Cynthia MacDonald Gamblin,
Daughter of General Contractor Robert MacDonald

MOST of my personal memories of the Arch come from the early years of its construction rather than the year of its completion. I was attending Randolph-Macon Women's College in Lynchburg, Virginia, during the critical last months and missed seeing the "Topping Off Ceremony" in person. It was my father, R.E. MacDonald, President of MacDonald Construction Company of St. Louis, known to his friends as Gene, who was awarded the contract for the construction of the Gateway Arch.

My father's primary reason for undertaking this project was the tremendous challenge that it presented to him personally as well as professionally. Everyone involved in bringing Eero Saarinen's grand design to fruition was challenged by the uniqueness of the Arch's construction. Many well-respected engineers and contractors of that era, including my father's own brother, himself also a civil engineer, said that it could not be accomplished. What others did not know about Daddy was the

strength, integrity and fortitude he had. This was a man who had gone to Africa and Italy to serve his country during World War II and had returned having been awarded the Order of the British Empire, a highly unusual commendation for an American. Whenever Mom or I would ask him for specifics as to why he was awarded the O.B.E., his comment was always, "Just for doing my job." To this day, I have no idea what that "job" entailed, but I imagine Daddy approached it as yet another challenge.

One amusing thing Daddy told me was that on several occasions he would be called down to the police station to bail out a few of his construction workers. They had been taunted about building the "Big Wicket" and came out swinging, landing themselves in jail. The joke going around was that the croquet ball would be built on the other side of the river, in East St. Louis.

After the Arch was completed and the challenge met, my father's greatest sense of accomplishment shifted from the reality of the Arch to the incredible safety record during the construction. Not

one construction worker was seriously injured, much less killed, although it had been predicted by the insurance companies that 13 would die. My father had a very deep sense of humility and a quiet pride, but it was this record of which he was most noticeably proud, as it concerned others, not himself. However, it did underscore the fact that his decision to use only skilled workers on the job had been a wise one. One organization in particular was upset because he had no novice workers on the project. He knew well the challenges the Arch would present and was determined to meet them appropriately and directly, in his own way.

LAYING THE FOUNDATIONS
Ted Rennison,
Engineer, Eero Saarinen and Associates

(Bottom) The hole for the Arch foundations having been dug, a massive concrete pour was made beginning June 27, 1962. This photo shows the open excavation for the south leg's foundation, which averaged 45 feet in depth, but plunged to 50 feet on the southeast side of the hole to reach bedrock. The initial pour took 23 hours and laid down 2,400 yards of concrete. The large "bucket" seen in the photo was attached to the crane cable. It was filled directly from a concrete truck which dumped its load into a hopper device built on the side of the bank, seen near the top center of the photo. The capacity of the trucks was 6 yards of concrete, enough to fill the bucket, which could then be swung by the crane to dump its load where needed.

(Top) A total of seven "pours," each 5 feet deep, were made to create each of the two foundation pads for the Arch. In order to make the pours interlock with one another, a keystoned series of grooves, looking much like the furrows made in a farmer's field by a plow, were created, as seen on the left of this photo. The excavation for the Arch footings was 75 feet wide and 90 feet long.

MY first day on the job in 1961 was in a snow storm as they were preparing the north footings for the railroad cut/tunnel which runs in front of the Arch. There was a good deal of careful selection of the colors in reference to the mortar in the big, curved levee floodwall. We went so far as to send various samples back to Saarinen in the main office for them to make their decision, even to the extent of sending four or five of the levee stones themselves for them to judge just what they wanted to use.

The money was not available at the time to put in the monumental entrance stairs which Saarinen had called the grand stairs. So that work was held back. However, we did put in the concrete support beams with a piling in the sloped area, and they were covered with dirt until such time, at a later date, that they could be used. If at any time the memorial decided to put in the balance of the stairs, the underground work was there for them. Saarinen, of course, wanted marble for the treads on the stairs, including an area that goes right across the levee road.

Next we began excavations for the Arch footings and the visitor center itself. And of course that was practically all blasting solid rock at the Arch footings. There were 32,000 yards of limestone rock taken out of the combined two footings, plus the load zones for the Arch Transportation System at each leg of the Arch. We poured the concrete roof of the museum and visitor center through the winter, and we had to do a lot of winter heating to protect the concrete while it was curing. We had one occurrence of an accident with a crane in the lobby area. We had been putting the beams up. Those beams ran 13 tons each, and they were precast, and they were placing them with this big Manitowoc crane. One of the gears on the boom went out, and it came down and hit one of the wing columns out in the lobby area, and fractured it, and the end of it came down and punched a hole in the roof. We had to make some repairs, and we had to remove that one column and rebuild it. The crane boom, of course, was a wreck.

When we poured the concrete for the Arch foundations we had a continuous monolithic pour, because naturally we didn't want a cold joint, we wanted good, solid concrete, so they had to add a retarder to control the set of the concrete. It took 1,700 yards of concrete for the south leg, which had a slightly larger opening or hole than the north, and it took 23 hours

to make that pour. As the concrete for the footings progressed, at 34 feet below ground level we started to install the 1-inch post-tension bars that would be used to stabilize the Arch as it was constructed. And then at 24 feet below ground level, we started another group. This, of course, meant that the loading of the bars in the Arch footing were not all concentrated at one point. There were a total of 252 bars placed in the two extrados (outside or back) corners of each leg. They then continued up through the Arch to the top of concrete.

(Left) The first foundation pour for the north leg had been completed by July 17, 1962, as shown in this photo. Workmen are seen busily erecting wooden forms for the creation of a triangular hole or "void" in the center of the foundation, measuring 30 feet on a side. As on the south leg, care was taken during the initial pour to ensure a continuous flow of concrete. Each pour resulted in a layer of concrete five feet deep; the concrete had to be laid in two rounds or "lifts." A layer of concrete two and one-half feet deep would be put down evenly within the bounds of the entire excavation, then a second layer of the same depth would be laid to equal the 5-foot depth. To prevent "a cold joint" between one lift and the next, which would weaken the structure, a "retarder" was added to the concrete mix to delay the setting of the concrete from three to four hours.

(Top) By August 22, 1962, the south leg's foundation was nearly complete and backfilled, although the wooden forms were still in place. A total of 252 steel post-tensioning rods in two clusters can be seen protruding from the concrete at the "extrados" corners on the right, at the back of the leg's foundation pad. The one and one-fourth-inch rods were held in place by steel plates with spacing holes drilled in them.

(Bottom) Near the top of the footing, horizontal post-tension bars were added to increase support across the 6 by 9-foot opening for the tram, seen at the bottom center of this photo. The final foundation pour was made on the north leg on October 2, 1962. A total of 12,000 yards of concrete comprise each of the foundation pads.

*T*he post-tensioning bars were the solution to one of the major engineering problems in constructing the Arch. How do you build a 630-foot arch, which like all arches since Ancient Rome depends upon the two sides exerting pressure on one another to stand up, with both sides pushing against a keystone at the center top? How do you build a gigantic arch and keep the sides from falling inward before you place the keystone? Some engineers suggested long guy wires stretching huge distances to the north and south of each leg, others towers of 700 feet tall balanced by guy wires to hold the legs back, but the final solution was the use of post-tensioning bars set into the concrete. These bars acted together with the concrete like the tendons in an arm or a leg, resisting gravity and holding back the curving legs. The bars had to be inclined in two directions to fit the curvature of the Arch as well as the tapering of the legs. Each bar was tensioned to 71 tons of pressure and continued to the top of concrete at 300 feet. When the Arch reached 530 feet, a gigantic strut was placed between the legs to ensure their stability and to take some of the pressure off the post-tensioned concrete. Weight, especially the weight on each leg during construction, was always a concern to the engineers, and everything from the weight of the creeper cranes to the number of personnel and tools on each leg was carefully considered.

Facts About the Construction
Joe Jensen,
Engineer, Associate Director,
National Park Service

Each leg of the Gateway Arch is an equilateral triangle with sides 54 feet long at ground level, tapering to 17 feet at the top. The legs have double walls of steel 3 feet apart at ground level and 7 ¾ inches apart above the 400-foot level. Up to the 300-foot mark the space between the walls is filled with reinforced concrete. Beyond that point steel stiffeners are used.

The double-walled triangular sections were placed one on top of another and then welded inside and out to build the legs of the Arch. Sections ranged in height from 12 feet at the base to 8 feet for the two keystone sections. The complex engineering design and construction is completely hidden from view. All that can be seen is its sparkling stainless steel outside skin and inner skin of carbon steel, which combine to carry the gravity and wind loads to the ground. The Arch has no real structural skeleton; and that is the essence of what is meant by "orthotropic" design. Its inner and outer steel skins, joined to form a composite structure, give it its strength and permanence.

Each group of tensioning bars required careful positioning because the bars had to be inclined in two directions – to fit the curvature of the Arch as well as the tapering cross-section of the legs. With the steelwork in place, concreting proceeded in lifts of about 5

This billboard-like sign stood throughout the construction on the Arch grounds. An official overlook was constructed to give visitors a chance to observe the construction at fairly close range from a designated safe point.

feet each. The bars were post-tensioned after the 5,000-psi concrete reached a strength of 4,000 psi - usually after seven to ten days.

The stressing was done by a hydraulic jack, which applied a load of 71 tons on each bar, or a total of 18,000 tons for each leg. Bars were tensioned in a strict sequence specified by the engineers. The full load was applied to each bar in one operation with a center-hole hydraulic jack of 100-ton capacity, which reacted against a steel jacking plate 1 $\frac{3}{4}$-inches thick embedded in the top of the concrete.

(Middle) On February 12, 1963, the foundation pad for the south leg was ready to receive the first steel section of the Gateway Arch. The first piece sits on a rail car used to shuttle sections from the welding shack to the construction. The section weighed 43 tons, stood 12 feet tall, measured 54 feet on a side, and had a 3-foot gap between the inner and outer steel skins. All of these dimensions would become smaller on successive sections as the Arch tapered gracefully toward the top.

(Top) After the first section was set, the post-tensioning rods and steel stiffeners were extended through it, and the 3-foot area between the outer skin of one-fourth-inch stainless steel and the inner skin of three-eighths-inch carbon steel was filled with concrete. This photograph shows the concrete work in progress, with a full bucket being swung into position.

(Bottom) The process of construction continued with the placement of the second section on the south leg on April 12, 1963. Completed sections were lifted by cranes and put into position 4 inches above the previously placed section, where they were set on three 35-ton jacks. The jacks were used to position the section accurately, leaving a gap between it and the one below it just wide enough for the welds. Over the next two and one-half years, piece by piece, section by section, the Gateway Arch would reach toward the sky, 71 sections composing each leg, for a total of 142.

Building the Cranes that Built the Arch
Russ Knox,
Oiler, Crane Operator

WHEN the Arch was first started I worked on the project as an oiler. It was my job to keep the crane up to snuff, keep it clean. When you see the old pictures now of the construction, you think, gee, were the trucks really that small, and was everything that old, and the overhead trestles, were they that shabby-looking? And the bums. There were little enclaves of bums that lived down there. It seems like they'd set up camp with little boxes in the wintertime in high grass out there and they'd have their little fires. I remember one occasion when a fellow came to work, and started up his bulldozer, and a body comes rolling out with the dirt. And it was a bum that had gone to sleep up against that dozer blade as a windbreak. Didn't kill him. The operator said the guy tumbled off to one side, but popped up like a cork, and ran like the dickens toward the Old Cathedral.

Just prior to the concrete pour for the Arch leg foundations, the master mechanic said to me one day, "We've got a crane coming in on a siding down there; they want it together tomorrow." This was mid-afternoon, and they wanted it on the job by 4:30 the next day. At the time I'd put a lot of cranes together. So I went down there and there were, I don't know how many flatcars, I want to say it was

seven, and this humongous crane, and a huge boom, that was all bolted down to the cars with huge bolts. And I thought it would take us four days just to unbolt this thing, much less put it together! So I went back up and I said, "Well, we need a crane, maybe two of them." So here we're going to take two cranes to put one together! And this particular crane, as I recall, was rated at 150 tons, which by the standards of those days was huge. It could probably pick up some of the bigger cranes that we had. And it was capable of a 300-foot boom. This was the 4000 Manitowoc Crane. And I think it was the biggest one that Manitowoc made, that could be called a conventional track crane. Anyway, we worked around the clock, and we had it on the job the next day. This was the crane that was used to pour the south leg of the Arch, the first footings.

It seems to me like we had practically everybody in St. Louis in on the project of supplying the concrete, because nobody, no one company, was set up to supply this much concrete, especially

Conventional cranes were used on the project throughout the construction process up to the point when the Arch legs reached 72 feet tall. Cranes were used to lift concrete into place for the pouring of the foundations. In this view, concrete trucks are lined up waiting to dump their loads into a bucket suspended from a crane in June 1962.

On February 12, 1963, the first section of the Gateway Arch is lifted into place by a Manitowoc crane, one of the largest made at that time. Conventional cranes like this one lifted the first six sections into place, up to a height of 72 feet. Beyond that point the specially conceived derrick cranes attached to the back of the Arch legs had to be utilized.

(Opposite page) Deliveries of concrete continued in colorful trucks like this one as the gap between the inner and outer skins of the Arch was filled, a process which continued up to the 300-foot level.

because so many other things, including the stadium, were also under construction. Anyway, that was a big morning, that first pour, everybody was there early. Gosh, I remember it being really exciting, when that first bucket of concrete came over. I guess it was really tantamount to breaking a champagne bottle on the bow of a ship. We're launching this thing officially this morning.

And of course the excitement kind of cools as the day goes on. As the sun comes up it gets a little hotter and it gets into a monoto-

ny by then. Every bucket that goes down at first, you are cheering. And then you're thinking, "My God! When are we going to quit this? How many yards have we got left?" It was so interesting to see that many trucks go that fast - the trucks couldn't keep up with the bucket, because you figured that every time that bucket came away from that platform, he had a truckload of concrete. He'd take it out, and all he had to do was set it down in there and pour it out.

The crane operators on this job were phenomenal. One of them could hand you a 50-foot beam that weighed 10 tons, could literally hand it to you, way up in the air and only being able to hear signals, or watch a guy make a hand signal. An operator had to be good; the story goes that operators that didn't have a lot of finesse could dust a guy off of a beam – it could happen – or get a little rough or a little careless. Not the ones we had on the Arch.

CRAWLING THROUGH THE CANS
Fred Morris,
Ironworker on the Arch Project

I worked for Donco and basically we put in all of the reinforcing on the Arch. I would get subbed out from Donco to MacDonald on the stress rods, greasing the stress rods when they were placed in the concrete. You would crawl through the cans [Arch sections] and grease them so when they poured the others and they put jacks on

Workmen inside the Arch can clearly be seen in this view, taken near the end of construction in 1965.

them and pulled the stress rods they would adhere to the concrete. Because it was such a dirty, greasy job they furnished everybody with blue coveralls. So they named us the "blue angels." It was not a heavenly job. You walked or crawled through these cans and you greased these rods and it was hot.

Once the site portion of it got to the point where they narrowed it down to just the Arch itself, you had the elevator constructors inside starting on the elevators, the sheet metal guys in there working on the duct work, the electricians coming in doing a lot of the electrical work, that type of thing. It was still pretty congested, but nothing like it was when the site work was going on.

The higher you got on it, that project was a job that not every ironworker wanted to work on. I've seen some really good ironworkers, I mean excellent ironworkers, come down after working on that thing for just a short time and say, "Hey, this ain't for me." Because everything was an illusion, you know, you're working inside a can. And the thing started leaning over at a degree and all of a sudden it looked like you could just step out and walk across but you couldn't because it was on a slant. And even though there weren't serious injuries, it was a scary deal for a lot of guys.

*B*oth legs of the Gateway Arch were erected simultaneously without scaffolding. The first few triangular sections, up to a height of 72 feet, were handled by conventional cranes operating from the ground. Above that height a derrick was affixed to the back of each of the legs of the Arch. Each derrick platform measured 43 by 32 feet; with a crane mounted on it the assembly weighed 100 tons. The derricks were used to raise the remaining 12-foot high, 50-ton sections.

Two vertical tracks held the sled that supported the derrick and platform. These tracks, made from 12 WF steel beams, were spaced 24 feet apart. Each track was attached to brackets held by four high-strength 1 ¼-inch diameter steel bolts. As the Arch increased in height, the derricks were moved up the tracks on the back of the curved legs of the Arch; the tracks were extended as sections were added and the Arch grew taller. Sections of track were added in 48-foot lengths,

and the entire derrick crept up after it had placed four sections of the Arch. The adjustable supports of the derricks kept them level with the horizon regardless of the height and curvature of the legs. Because the height eventually made it difficult for workmen to climb to and from the work area, the derricks were reached by a passenger elevator and were equipped with a tool shed for workmen, sanitary facilities, and communications equipment.

The derricks were operated from sheds on the ground. The operators followed the instructions of a signal man who was located either on the derrick platform or at the top of the leg, depending upon the purpose of the lift being made. Signalman and operator communicated via telephones. Lifting an Arch section into place took about a half-hour. The derricks also lifted concrete, supplies, parts for the interior stairways, trams and other items as needed.

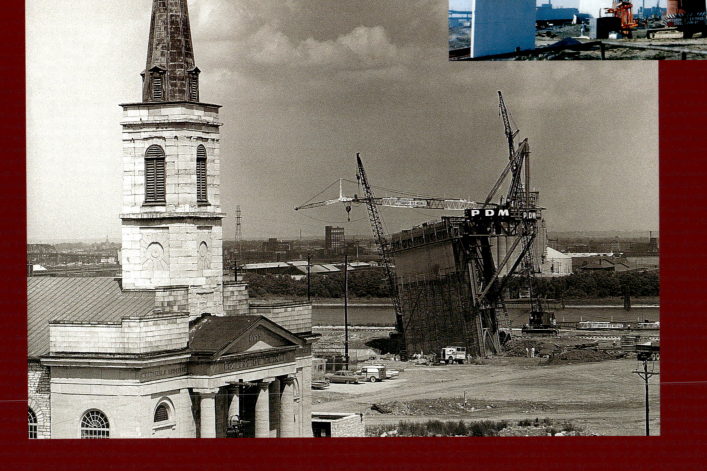

(Opposite page) Rails were placed on the back of the Arch to allow the creeper derricks to move upward with the Arch as it grew. The rails were set with anchor bolts that went through the stainless steel skin of the Arch and were anchored in the concrete. Above 300 feet the bolts were carried through to the inner skin. Knee braces under the derrick platform were adjustable, so that it was always in a vertical position. Every time the derrick was raised to a new station, it was lifted 40 feet.

(Bottom) The Old Cathedral stands nearby as the Arch, now fitted with a creeper derrick, continues to move skyward. Soon this 1834 house of worship would be dwarfed by its neighbor, an immense rainbow of stainless steel.

(Top) As the Arch grew taller, it was found that a section could not be raised if the winds were over 30 miles per hour. A gauge on the Arch was used to judge wind speed. If a section was raised above the top of the Arch on a blustery day, and the wind took it, it could also topple the derrick.

CHAPTER 5

PROGRESS AND PROTESTS

1964

(Top) A stainless steel-clad section is carefully lowered into place during 1964. As each section was placed, many adjustments had to be made in order to make the sections fit properly and enable a proper weld.

(Bottom) President Lyndon B. Johnson visited St. Louis on February 14, 1964 on the occasion of the Bicentennial of the City of St. Louis. During his tour of the city he briefly visited the construction site of the Gateway Arch, and was shown plans and a comparative height chart by city and National Park Service officials. Several of the workers were able to shake hands with the President and listen to a short speech.

*D*uring 1964 great progress was made on the Gateway Arch. For those workers who labored steadily on the project, the incredible nature of what they were building, its uniqueness and its unprecedented engineering, made their daily tasks seem special indeed. At the end of February, the south leg stood at 168 feet, the north at 204 feet. Questions arose, prompted by several outside firms and agencies, regarding the unique nature of the engineering. Many engineers said that the Arch was improperly designed and would not stand when completed, but engineers from the Severud firm were able to withstand these critiques and prove to the satisfaction of most engineers that their calculations were sound. The project was so unique that some had to wait until the structure was completed and saw it standing on its own to be convinced.

WILL THE ARCH STAND?
George B. Hartzog, Jr.,
Director, National Park Service, 1964-1972

PARTWAY through the project, Pittsburgh-Des Moines Steel Company (PDM) concluded that without modification the Arch would fall down when the last section was lifted to close the 630-foot high Arch. That news scared the liver out of Secretary of the Interior Stewart Udall and me. We had the major memorial project in the whole world underway, and the contractor said it was going to fall down.

With LBJ as president, such an event would surely present limitations on your future. I could see if the damn thing fell, the first guy out the door was me. So, I met with Mr. Fred Severud, and with Hanskarl Bandel, and Joe Jensen, NPS Associate Director for Design and Construction (a former partner of Eero Saarinen) and Mr. William R. Jackson (CEO) and his engineers and consultants of Pittsburgh-Des Moines Steel (PDM). PDM's lead advocate was a university professor who was an expert on engineering design and theory. We met in my conference room in the Main Interior Building in Washington. I listened to those guys as they went back and forth with esoteric theories, stuff I'd never even begin to understand. Finally, Fred Severud said to the professor, "Doctor, you know we are imposing on Mr. Hartzog because I don't think he understands what we're talking about. Now the only way I know to resolve this argument is to build a model and wind tunnel test it. If it survives the

test we're not issuing any change order. You pay for the test. If it fails the test, I'll pay for the test and I will recommend a change order. Goodbye."

The professor did not reply. He started reaching for his papers, folding them up, and slipped them in his briefcase. I figured right then that the argument was over. We got up, shook hands, and Mr. Severud left. After they had departed, I said to Joe Jensen, "How much did Severud put on the line?" He said, "That would cost about $1 million." That sure did fortify my confidence in Fred's opinion.

But PDM was not through with the argument. They hired Gen. Donald Dawson, a distinguished Washington lawyer, who had been a military aide to President Truman, to take their appeal to Secretary Udall. Udall listened to General Dawson and to Bill Jackson, president of PDM, and to me. The Secretary promised to look into the matter. When they had departed, he told me that he thought he should have the engineers of the Bureau of Reclamation assess the dispute. I protested that they did not have a single engineer that I knew of that was qualified in orthotropic design and that the argument was really about which of

(Bottom) The role of engineers in the success of the Gateway Arch project can never be overestimated. Engineering work continued to be of great importance while the project was underway. In this photo, Pittsburgh-Des Moines engineers Gordon Warner and Ken Kolkmeier are seen taking a night reading with a theodolite scope. As the Arch progressed, each night after a new section was placed, triangulation shots would be taken to ensure the accuracy of the placement. They were taken at night because the temperature was more constant; as the Arch grew taller, the heat of the sun skewed the legs a few inches out of alignment each day. Target lights were placed at three corners of the Arch section, and readings could be taken from the east side and the west side of the structure. If the structure was off by a fraction of an inch, it increased the chances that the entire leg would be so far out of alignment by the time it reached the top of the Arch that it would not meet the other leg properly. Measurements resulted in the subtle repositioning of sections prior to welding.

(Top) Gordon Warner and Ken Kolkmeier go over their night readings and calculate changes to the set of a section of the Arch.

two engineering theories was valid and appropriate in this instance. He was insistent, however, that you've got to have something more than the consultant that has a vested interest. I retained the Bureau of Reclamation at a cost of $100,000 to do the analysis.

Shockingly, they agreed with PDM.

When Secretary Udall got the report he called me into his office. In the meantime Joe Jensen and Fred Severud had been advised of the bureau's report and their opinion was that it was $100,000 worth of bunk! Moreover, Severud told me that if we accepted the bureau's conclusion and issued PDM the change order he would withdraw from the project. The Secretary was clearly worried that a major bureau of his department had told him that I was leading him into a debacle, and that the Arch was going to fall down if he didn't approve the change order. I had just told him that if he issued the change order, we would have to complete the Arch without Severud, and, importantly, Bandel, who was the only engineer then readily available who had worked with orthotropic structures.

I said to Stewart as we both paced the floor of his huge, ornate office, "You can always get another director but, in my judgment, Severud is irreplaceable. Why don't you let me stay on course? If it comes out OK, you are home free. If the damn thing falls down, fire me, have a news conference and announce the appointment of another director to clean up the mess!"

Before he could respond, the buzzer went off on his desk. He answered, listened and said, "Just the man I need to see, send him in."

In walked Nat Owings, senior partner of Skidmore, Owings and Merrill, one of America's most distinguished architects. Without even inquiring about the purpose of his visit, Stewart immediately began to outline the problem he and I had been discussing. When he finished, I then told Nat my proposition to let me stay the course and if it fell down, to fire me and have another director clean up the mess.

Stewart asked, "Nat, what do you think we should do?"

Nat began, "I have known Fred Severud for many years - he is one of the best. He challenged them to a test and they didn't take it. I'd do what George suggests. If he's wrong, fire him."

Nat Owings, through an incredible coincidence, had saved Eero Saarinen's Arch.

I went back downstairs, called General Dawson, and told him that the Secretary had just given me full responsibility for the decision. "We are not going to issue any change order; PDM should proceed in accordance with the plans."

About this time, the Secretary had asked me to participate in a team study of historic preservation in Europe. My wife Helen and I arrived in New York to join the group prior to departure. We were staying at the Pierre Hotel. About 9:30 that night I received a telephone call from Bill Jackson of PDM, once again pressing for a change order. He insisted that the Arch was going to fall down when they lifted the final section.

My response was, "Lift it, Mr. Jackson; if she falls, I'm fired."

Pittsburgh-Des Moines Steel engineer Mike Schuller (right) uses a model to make calculations on the Arch structure.

(Left) There are 886 tons of one-fourth-inch stainless steel on the outside of the Arch. The steel is Type 304 with a #3 finish. Half of the stainless steel came from U.S. Steel, the other half from Industrial Stainless Steel, a division of Eastern Stainless Steel Corporation of Baltimore, Maryland. The inner skin is of A-7 carbon steel. The welding of all of this steel was critical in building an orthotropic structure like the Gateway Arch.

(Right) Being an expert welder was not the only criteria for working on the Arch project, for, as can be seen from these photos, the welder could have no fear of heights. The polished stainless steel plates were joined using MIG (metal inert gas) welding with an automatic electrode head, utilizing a shielding mixture of 75% argon and 25% carbon dioxide. Electrolytic cleaning removed the halos on the stainless steel caused by the heat of welding.

(Opposite page, top) A semiautomatic Bugo welder was used for a short time at the beginning of the Arch project. It ran along a rack arrangement and was geared to the welding unit. The operators could control the speed of the wire and the speed of the travel of this device as it went along. The arc was shielded with neon gas to prevent any possibility of the oxidation of the weld. It was thought that the machine would enable a faster and more consistent weld, but the welders themselves found over the course of time that their skilled work was better in every way than what the machine could do on a project such as the Gateway Arch.

(Opposite page, bottom) Long shadows of the Arch legs signal the end of another day on the project. Welding took place on the ground as well as at the top of the completed work, for the Arch sections were shipped in parts which had to be welded together on a weather-protected concrete welding pad. After welding was completed on the ground, a conventional crane lifted a completed section onto a specially designed railroad car with a 42 by 52-foot deck and an outrigger with rubber-tired wheels to support the third corner of the gigantic steel triangles. The railroad car made a trip over a short stretch of tracks to a position where the section could be lifted into place by one of the creeper derricks.

WELDING TRYOUTS
Ted Rennison,
Engineer, Eero Saarinen and Associates

ACH man who came here had to have a background in welding through his union. And they had to take a very elaborate test. A lot of men didn't use, or had never used the type of rod that we were going to use here. We used a low-hydrogen rod. In my opinion, it makes a good deal better or smoother weld, and a better-appearing weld, than some of the others. These men had to go to a lab and take the tests. The tests were quite rigid; there was a vertical and horizontal and overhead. We had many people come here from the local ironworker's union, and they took the test and passed. For some reason, we had quite a turnover among the local ironworkers from this union. And then we ended up with the majority of the people that were doing the welding coming from Arkansas. They were pipeline workers, and did welding on gas lines and oil lines throughout the country. These fellows were very good, and to my knowledge, I think there was only one or two of the local men who stayed throughout the job. Apparently they didn't care for the type of work we had, because it was very confining. They were in a closed area where they had to take the reflection of the heat and the dirt that occurs in welding. The pipeline men were more accustomed to it, and it didn't bother them as much.

74

Russ Knox,
Oiler, Crane Operator

THE welders got three days to do demonstration welds. I saw welders there that would certainly be categorized as crafts-men. These guys could strike an arc, and the consistency of the arc, the color, the sound, was incredible. You could hear the governors on gas-operated generators, on welders. On the governors, as the surge changed from the rod tip to the steel, the governor might fluc-tuate a little bit. These were the kind of guys who would strike an arc, and the RPM on that welder engine would stay exactly the same. In other words, they could control that head carefully. And the work that they did, it was such a beautiful job. And so many of these guys were rejected. Guys who thought that they did magnificent work. But they were going to be called upon to do some stainless steel stuff. Later on, as they put the sections of the Arch itself together, they put a track, a machine, on the side, and they welded the plates together with a machine, with an automatic feed, which was some-thing that was relatively new at the time. They had the best people doing the best possible work, which made the outcome inevitable. When you are on a project like that, the people who are sloppy, and the people who have attitudes, they don't stay. They are gone. Because you have to work together.

WORKING FROM THE INSIDE
Fred Morris,
Ironworker on the Arch Project

I worked for Southwest Ornamental Iron Works on the interior. We were building the platforms, handrails, stairs, all of the structures, steel and everything inside all the way up, the supporting rails for the cars, the capsules and all of that. The process was that the derricks were used by the guys from PDM that were "stacking cans" [hoisting sections into place] during the week. So we would come in on the weekends and hoist our material inside the Arch with the derricks. That was a very interesting thing in itself and the higher you got the more interesting it got: because you're trying to feed in structural steel, long stair stringers, 20-foot sections of handrail and everything through the mouth of this leg of the Arch. It is laying over and over more and more, and you're trying to wrestle this stuff down and set it down some place. Most of the time we were working six days a week. Once in awhile we got the seventh day in when we got to the welding part, to make sure we stayed up with the can crew, you know, those guys outside. Most of the time you'd pair up with another welder, because you can imagine if you just had to keep your head under that hood all day.

One time, one of the guys hung a thermometer inside that Arch in the summertime in August, and if I remember right it was almost 150 degrees in that thing. You'd come out and your boots would be wringing wet. Most of the time, if you opened the doors at the bottom there would be a natural draft coming through there. It would help cool it down in the summer and it would freeze your butt off in the winter. Someone would open that door in the winter and you'd hear everybody scream.

An idea of the crowded conditions on and inside an Arch leg can be gained from this photo, showing a section being lowered into place on the rising structure.

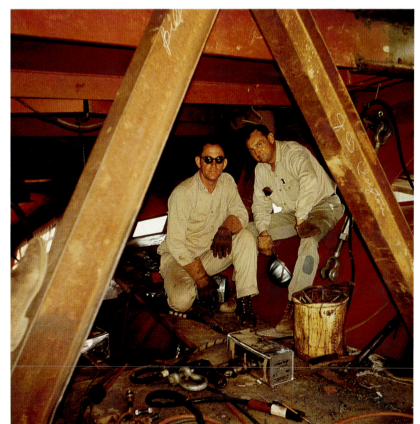

(Top) Cramped conditions inside the Gateway Arch were made worse when workmen installed conduit and motor generator units for the tram system beneath the decking of the observation area at the top.

(Bottom left) Two workmen labor within the confines of the interior of the unfinished Arch.

(Bottom right) A complete set of emergency access stairs was installed in each leg of the Arch. Since each winding set of 1,076 steps must follow the curves of the structure and occupy only half of the triangular interior in the upper portions of the structure, an elaborate series of curves and angles had to be devised. The stairs were installed as the Arch was constructed.

Not all of the stories connected with the Arch are happy or uplifting ones. One of the major tragedies in our nation's history, racism, played a part in the Arch story as well. In the shadow of the Old Courthouse, where the Dred Scott case had begun 100 years earlier, very few African-Americans were employed on the project to build the Arch. Since the Arch was built in the midst of the Civil Rights era, during which sit-ins, freedom riders, protests, and rousing speeches by such leaders as Dr. Martin Luther King, Jr. and Malcolm X reverberated throughout the land, it was inevitable that the Arch project would receive not just criticism, but active protests. The passage of the Civil Rights Act of 1964 and the Voting Rights Act of 1965 left the leaders of various civil rights groups seeking new rallying points. While some Americans worried that the rights of the ordinary citizen were being dictated by an intrusive government, others wanted to try to repair the damage of hundreds of years of racial oppression.

One of the major civil rights problems was high unemployment among people of color, and the inability of African-Americans, due to discriminatory practices in many employment fields, to work in certain types of jobs and crafts. Workers in the construction trades were difficult if not impossible to coerce into adopting equal employment opportunity, since they were not hired from the street but by low bid contractors from union halls under prior and exclusive work contracts. One starting point was to pursue lucrative federal government contracts and construction jobs. In St. Louis, the problem was vexing and difficult to attack except by some dramatic, confrontational gesture which would generate publicity and embarrass the federal government, its contractors and more particularly the trades unions on the high-profile Arch project into reevaluating their hiring practices.

Activists Percy Green and Richard Daly are seen chained to the framework of the work ladder on the south leg of the Arch during their protest of July 14, 1964. When workmen returned from their lunch break, they could not use the blocked ladder. Green and Daly shouted their demands to the astounded workers, 120 feet below, insisting that at least 10% of the Arch workforce should be African-American. The stalemate ended when police cut the chains and led the two men down the ladder to face federal charges.

THE GATEWAY ARCH PROTEST, JULY 14, 1964
Percy Green, Civil Rights Activist

WHEN the Gateway Arch was under construction and stood at the 300-foot level in the summer of 1964, an activist element of the civil rights organization known as the Congress of Racial Equality (CORE), which soon after organized as the Action Council to Improve Opportunities for Negroes (ACTION), was successful in protesting the banking industry in St. Louis for fair employment for African-Americans.

Afterwards, this activist element began searching for another institution to attack that was guilty of racial discrimination. They did not have to look far. They learned from the newspapers that federal dollars were being spent to build the Gateway Arch.

When the activists sent out their investigating team, made up of both black and white members, to the Arch site to see what was going on, we found there were no black contractors and very few black workers. In fact, none of the black workers were in skilled positions, such as crane operators, carpenters, ironworkers, or cement masons. The few that were visible were laborers. We spoke to the general contractor, MacDonald Construction Company, about our findings. The contractor said that they had tried but could not find qualified black contractors to do some of the work. Regarding skilled workers, the contractor said that there were only a few blacks and they were all working on other construction jobs, and that the unions were responsible for the fact that there were so few skilled black construction workers.

We did not find these excuses acceptable. The question became: How could we expose to the world that this national monument, the Arch, which was under construction, was guilty of racial discrimination using federal tax dollars?

During a strategy session, it was determined that an exploratory reconnaissance was necessary. There were two volunteers. Richard Daly, a European-American, joined me, an African-American, to test the waters by seeing how far we could explore the Arch site without confrontation. A few days later we visited the site at lunchtime. We were dressed like construction workers, in Levis, T-shirts, and boots. We walked up to the north leg of the Arch, and seemed to be viewed as regular workers. We walked around the grounds and left without incident.

At the next strategy session, we reported our experience, and after some discussion, a direct-action protest plan was adopted. We decided to climb the Arch to expose the fact that federal funds were being used to build a national monument that was racially discriminating against black contractors and black skilled workers. For the greatest possibility of success, the same two activists (Dick Daly and myself) volunteered to climb the Arch.

On July 14, 1964, as a diversionary tactic, ACTION announced to the news media that it would be picketing at the Old Courthouse at Market and Broadway about racial discrimination at the Arch. The Old Courthouse housed the offices of the National Park Service, the federal agency that was building the Arch. Binoculars were in place at the Old Courthouse for the public to view the construction at the Arch site. The picket line was set up at 10 a.m.

At noon the two of us, dressed like construction workers, again approached the Arch site. We walked by the workers having lunch to the ladder on the north leg of the Arch. We climbed to the 125-foot level and sat there, a safe distance from the workers above.

After observing through the binoculars at the Old Courthouse that we had in fact successfully climbed the Arch and were in position, Robert Curtis, an African-American attorney, informed the media that was covering the picket line. They immediately ran down to the Arch grounds for pictures of the climbers and to get the story. We remained on the Arch for six hours. When we came down we were arrested by the St. Louis Police Department and charged with trespassing on federal property and resisting arrest, because we refused to walk to jail.

A week or so later, it was announced publicly by the National Park Service that the general contractor had let work to three black firms. All of the arrest charges against us were dropped by the federal government in Washington D.C.

Green and Daly are seen in this photo talking with the press, workmen, and city and federal officials, including park superintendent Leroy Brown in the "smokey bear" hat. Percy Green, a former aerospace worker and employment committee chairman with CORE, formed ACTION in 1964 and specialized in high-profile, nonviolent protests of this type. Politicians and community figures, including the local newspapers, lambasted Green and Daly as mere publicity seekers, but the condemnations focused yet more attention on the Arch and the lack of a diversified workforce.

The First Pattern or Practice Equal Employment Opportunity Suit

The July 1964 protest was not the end of the Arch's role in the civil rights movement. As construction progressed on the Arch and new contracts were signed, the National Park Service was careful to stipulate that African-Americans would be expected to be part of the skilled work force. Park Superintendent LeRoy Brown told the St. Louis Globe-Democrat on October 29, 1964 that he had "indicated to the NAACP, the Urban League and CORE [that] we will accept only a contractor who has demonstrated he will be in full compliance."

When the Park Service opened bids for the construction of the visitor center under the Arch in the summer of 1965, the low bidder was Hoel-Steffen Construction Company, which pledged to follow equal employment opportunity practices. The St. Louis Building and Trades Union Council, AFL-CIO, however, declared that they would not work where AFL-CIO journeymen and apprentices were not used. Even if the AFL-CIO unions were sincere in pledging their support for equal opportunity employment, the construction trades in St. Louis still had no African-American craftsmen, and no programs were in place to recruit or hire any. In addition, alternative unions such as the Congress of Independent Unions (CIU), which was integrated, were being shut out of government contracts by the actions of the Building and Construction Trades Council.

Under heavy pressure from the U.S. Labor Department, Hoel-Steffen Construction Company hired the independent E. Smith Plumbing Company, a three-person African-American firm which was a member of the CIU. The appearance of the Smith company in the Gateway Arch visitor center on January 7, 1966 to install plumbing in the rest rooms triggered a walkout by five locals of the Building and Construction Trades

Council, who charged that the CIU members were unfair competitors. Work stopped entirely on the Gateway Arch visitor center for over a month. The National Park Service under the guidance of Compliance Officer, Woody Zenfell, was dedicated to the ideals of affirmative action, and had no notion of removing the Smith firm to appease the AFL-CIO. Hoel-Steffen found themselves caught between the federal government's push for equal employment opportunity and the all-white building and construction trades unions. The AFL-CIO construction trades locals maintained their fight was over a union-busting move by the U.S. Government. African-American St. Louisans rallied to push their fight for greater representation in the building trades.

On February 3, 1966, at a National Labor Relations Board hearing, the trade union walkout at the Gateway Arch triggered the first "pattern or practice suit" for discrimination in hiring filed by the Justice Department under Title VII of the Civil Rights Act of 1964. After a ruling that the Building and Construction Trades Council and four member unions were engaging in a secondary boycott at the Arch site, the workers went back to work on February 9.

In later litigation, the U.S. Court of Appeals overturned a lower court decision, and asserted that the Civil Rights Act of 1964 provided that employers "follow racially neutral employment policies" and maintain an "obligation to correct or revise practices which would perpetuate racial discrimination." The incidents at the Arch and the resulting litigation had an immediate positive effect on some St. Louis building trades unions, and as a result, apprenticeship programs were extended to African-American participation. The extraordinary protest at the Gateway Arch on July 14, 1964 by Percy Green and Richard Daly dramatized employment restrictions and led to a government response that resulted in the first direct actions of the federal government to enforce equal employment opportunity nationwide.

(Opposite page) As the Arch rose on the St. Louis riverfront, here glimpsed from beneath the Eads Bridge, important questions were raised during the mid-1960s about what the structure symbolized and who it benefited.

(Left) As the top of the area of concreting reached the 300-foot level, procedures changed. Post-tensioning rods were discontinued, and steel stiffeners maintained a constant gap between inner and outer walls.

(Right) Unassembled parts of sections sit on girders awaiting assembly on the welding pad. The Arch was like a complex jigsaw puzzle. Each piece of each Arch section was unique, because the Arch continually tapered inward, and the height and the length of the triangular sides was reduced as the pieces progressed upward. Also, because the Arch curved inward, the back of each triangular section was taller than the two inner pieces.

(Right) The workmen's elevator can be seen in this view, beneath the creeper derrick. As the height of the Arch increased, the amount of time it took for workmen to reach their work stations also became greater. By the end of the project it took up to 12 minutes to travel up the outside of the structure. The Marshall work elevator could hold four to five men and had a self-correcting leveling device. The final 10-40 feet of the climb, depending upon the position of the creeper derrick, had to be negotiated by ladder.

(Left) The number of concrete trucks on the work site, such as these photographed in January 1964, was greatly reduced after the Arch reached the 300-foot mark and was no longer reinforced between the inner and outer skins with concrete.

(Left and right) As construction topped the 300-foot mark workmen found their job site was often a lofty perch with a fine view of the city. Groups of dedicated and highly-skilled men continued to face the problems at hand: to safely, efficiently and professionally go about their ordinary daily tasks in an effort to raise an extraordinary and unique structure.

(Opposite page) Although the Arch still had over a year of construction left to go, the citizens of St. Louis turned out in large numbers to celebrate the Fourth of July on the riverfront in 1964. The tradition has continued until the present day, first with large fireworks displays and later with the Fair Saint Louis event, which began in 1981.

(Left) At the 300-foot mark, the top of concrete, each leg of the Arch was leaning in 49 feet from the vertical. At the point where the stabilizing strut was placed (530 feet) it was leaning in 150 feet. The tremendous weight and stress on the post-tensioned concrete and iron bars resulted from the loading of the Arch leg as it leaned, plus the 50-ton derrick on the back of it.

(Right) As the Arch increased in height, panoramic views of the city and the Mississippi River opened up; it soon became the tallest structure in the city. In this photo, the crane operator's "shack" can be seen as a white square just to the right of the south leg. The operator listened to a spotter on top of the Arch and controlled the movements of the derrick and cables from the shack on the ground.

(Right) Workmen smile as yet another section is lowered into place on the Arch. Conditions at the top varied from freezing cold winters to stiflingly hot summers. The one constant was the wind, which increased in ferocity the higher the Arch grew.

(Left) A train makes its way through the railroad tunnels and cuts in front of the Arch. The steel section pieces for the Arch were brought to the site from Pennsylvania by railroad, and could easily be unloaded by crane from a spot just below the Arch.

87

(Left) Workmen load lengths of iron into the interior of the Arch; while the outside progressed, the inside was also under construction, with elements of the tracks for the passenger tram, the electrical system, the heating and air conditioning ductwork and the work/emergency stairs all being installed.

(Right) Filling in between the inner and outer walls of the Arch took about 60 yards of concrete per section as the Arch approached 300 feet; the lifts were made with 3-yard buckets like the one shown here.

(Opposite page) Through 1964, the Gateway Arch continued to rise along the St. Louis riverfront, now looking much like two gigantic tusks reaching up out of the ground toward the sky. Old meets new in this picture, as a replica of a traditional Mississippi River steamboat passes the rising Arch.

CHAPTER 6

COMPLETION OF A DREAM

1965

*A*s the calendar turned to 1965, excitement began to build in St. Louis. The two legs of the Arch were growing ever higher and making a perceptible curve inward toward one another. The jeers and criticism of the "big wicket" on the riverfront turned to fondness and praise, as St. Louis began to receive national recognition and cover stories in such magazines as National Geographic and Life. The major problems with constructing the Arch all seemed in the past as the legs rose ever higher toward their ultimate union. School children began to write their names on "signatory sheets" which were collected for eventual inclusion in a "time capsule," an oblong metal box which was eventually welded inside the final Arch section. The climax came on October 28, 1965, as an American flag was placed on the final piece, and the last "can" was hauled skyward.

COULD THE ARCH BE BUILT TODAY?
Robert W. Duffy,
Journalist; Art and Architecture Critic,
St. Louis Post-Dispatch

ON October 28, 1965, the final section of the Gateway Arch was fitted into place, and one of human history's most potent works of art was completed. Ever since, the world has regarded it as the symbol of St. Louis and Americans recognize it as the Gateway to the West, a symbol of our manifest destiny.

What an accomplishment; what a grand and marvelous success! Could we do it again? Would we?

Joseph Shaughnessy, one of St. Louis' most respected and experienced builders and chairman of BSI Constructors, says the work could be accomplished today, in spite of the fact that building procedures related to safety have changed dramatically.

In the 40 years since the topping off of the Arch, concerns - and legal protection - for worker safety has gone from afterthought to a central issue in all places of employment and industry.

The Occupational Safety and Health Act established firm rules to protect the working men and women of the country and it is rigorously enforced. By some formula or another, it was estimated that a total of 13 unlucky construction workers would die. One such worker, aware of this ominous prediction, said five nights a week he went home, had dinner, went to bed and tried not to think about what he was doing. As it happened, not a single worker perished.

In the 1960s, Joe Shaughnessy – who would establish his own company in December, 1972 – watched the construction process with great interest and even climbed up the south leg of the monument with a group of construction company executives. He said recently that OSHA rules, which require such precautions as connecting the worker to a lifeline, might momentarily cramp a worker's style, but in the long run he or she would get used to it.

Building a structure such as the Arch, he said, "is not unlike building a bridge over a river and this could be done in such a way that would be unequivocally safe and would satisfy OSHA."

Shaughnessy said, however, that advancements in technology between now and then have not made building a structure such as the Arch any easier. It would be a challenge, but it could indeed be done.

So we could, but would we? Or should we?

The decision to build the monument, the harnessing of the civic and political acquiescence on the local and federal levels, the accumulation of the necessary clout to clear to the ground a 90-acre swath of an American city, the courage to look beyond the St. Louis architectural establishment and to mount an international competition, the will to opt for a design that transcends style and upsets tradition - would we be able successfully to juggle all those balls today?

Perhaps. Recent history, however, suggests to us the obstacles faced by a 21st century monument builder are monumental themselves.

Some are philosophical.

In the 21st century, should we make wholesale clearances of our built past, tearing down building after building that connects us visually and materially to our ancestors? Should we spend the money, put lives in jeopardy, rip up the architectural fabric to celebrate what can certainly be regarded as imperialism on the march? Can we honor the achievements of our European-blooded ancestors when they accomplished so much at the expense, or even the extermination, of so many native peoples?

If those gnawing questions were answered to the satisfaction of all, would the men and women of St. Louis from all backgrounds come together amicably with sufficient visual and intellectual and strategic resources to call an international competition and to put politics aside and choose the best design of the greatest architect, not a design that has broad popular appeal by a local architect with solid social and business connections? My guess, sadly, is that it is doubtful we could harness all those resources.

In the decades since the dedication of the Arch, we have maintained a tradition of willy-nilly and often purposeless land clearance, with no noble buildings or monuments to replace what has vanished. Buildings of international significance, such as Louis Sullivan's Wainwright Building, have come face to face with the wreckers. Unlike Sullivan, unlike Saarinen, the architectural establishment and its clientele here look to the past for patterns, not for inspiration, all too often.

Many mornings I run across the Eads Bridge to Illinois and back to St. Louis. I make the journey not simply for exercise but also for the pleasures that redound from connecting with that magisterial span, an act of architecture that is connected to the Arch by its shape, form and a shared sense of daring. I rejoice in the energy and the tension that crackle between the two. I look from bridge to Arch with delight.

But some days, although I rejoice in our good fortune for living in the shadow of this Arch, I am tormented by a suspicion that we no longer have what it takes to do it again.

In mid-July, 1965, as the Gateway Arch neared completion, many other major building projects were also underway, transforming the downtown area of St. Louis into a recharged, vital part of the city once more. In the lower center of the photo the 1874 Eads Bridge can be seen. Both the bridge and the Arch were seen as audacious engineering projects, each pushing the envelope in their own time for their design, use of materials, and construction methods.

DOCUMENTING THE ARCH

As the Arch continued to rise and the two legs began to curve inward to meet one another during 1965, the process of documenting the astounding feat was carried on by some very intrepid photographers and filmmakers.

Robert Arteaga and Art Witman were the principal still cameramen to chronicle the Arch's progress. Witman joined the St. Louis Post-Dispatch as a news photographer in 1932, and was one of the pioneers in the use of 35mm cameras in news photography in the mid 1930s. In addition to the Arch's construction, Witman documented Winston Churchill's 1946 "Iron Curtain" speech in Fulton, Missouri, Ku Klux Klan revivals in Georgia, Buckminster Fuller's geodesic Climatron at the Missouri Botanical Garden and the presidential campaigns of FDR, Truman, Eisenhower and Adlai Stevenson. Witman visited the Arch construction site frequently from 1963 to 1967. He was the only news photographer on permanent assignment at the construction. He also had complete access at the site and took photographs from all heights and angles. Witman shot mostly slides, but also used a Panox camera which covered 140 degrees of space horizontally.

In 1948 Robert Arteaga saw the first rendering of the Gateway Arch, which captured his imagination so strongly that he adopted the symbol as his business trademark long before the Arch was actually built. With his studio located on Third Street, directly across from the memorial grounds and the Old Cathedral, Arteaga had spent many years chronicling the historic buildings of the downtown area and the site of the Arch. In 1959 Arteaga was selected as the official project photographer by the MacDonald Construction Company. From the time that construction began with the railroad relocation project and continuing through the end of major contracts in 1967, Arteaga worked to record on film every step of the process, enduring harsh weather conditions and dizzying heights. Robert and his sons, Eldon and Wayne, tirelessly climbed the Arch each week with the construction crews. The record of each step and nuance of the process of building the Arch which was created by the Arteaga studio is the single greatest existing archive of images documenting this process.

Without the incredible photographic documentation of Robert Arteaga and Art Witman, the Gateway Arch project would not have been preserved for posterity in the detail it was. The photographs in this book are but a small sample of their important and visually stunning contribution to our nation's heritage through preserving, on film, images of this project.

In addition to still photography, a special documentary film was commissioned by the National Park Service to detail the construction of the Arch. The film was helmed by Charles Guggenheim, who won academy awards for his documentary works, Nine from Little Rock, Robert Kennedy Remembered, The Johnstown Flood, and A Time for Justice.

(Opposite page) Newspaper photographer Art Witman (seen here kneeling on top of the Arch) was self-motivated in his desire to chronicle the building of the Gateway Arch. Project Manager Ted Rennison recalled: "The man was not too far away from retiring. And he'd climb up that ladder from where the man-operated elevator would stop. Anything from 60 to 100 feet or so, bundles of photography equipment on his back. And he was so expert in his job, that he had extension poles, and he'd take pictures of something, that after you looked at them, you'd think you were standing out in the free air. He had an interesting experience: he dropped a Nikon from the top; about $2,500 worth of camera was ruined."

Posing with their photographic equipment in front of the recently completed Arch, the work of Robert Arteaga (left) and his sons Wayne and Eldon (right) comprised the most detailed and comprehensive photographic record of the construction. Crane operator Bill Quigley recalled: "It seemed like these fellows fell in love with the project. They started to take a couple of pictures, but then they couldn't put their doggone cameras down, and they just kept on taking pictures and pictures and pictures."

FILMING FROM A GREAT HEIGHT
Charles Guggenheim,
Filmmaker, *Monument to the Dream*

Filmmaker Charles Guggenheim, seen here in three images taken atop the Arch, headed a dedicated team of documentarians who chronicled the rise of the Arch. Producer T. Iglehart, editor Pierre Vacho, and cameramen Art Fillmore, Bob Pierce, Jack Richards, Bobby Bauer and Dick Duncan worked under sometimes perilous conditions to create a memorable film record of the Arch story.

I remember having a meeting in the Old Courthouse in 1961 about making a film of the Arch construction. George Hartzog and I got along very well, and George said "We're going to get this thing made." He had no federal funds for the film, so, as only Hartzog can do, he got the American Iron and Steel Institute, which was at that time a fairly formidable organization, interested in putting up funds for this, because it was the largest order of stainless steel that had ever been made, and maybe still is. And I suggested that they bring in Laclede Gas Company to put up some of the money, too. George Hartzog is one of the most remarkable people that has ever served in this government, because he would find some way to cut through any type of red tape or bureaucracy or procedural intimidation to get the job done.

In terms of my concepts for the film, there are a couple of things that always intrigued me. One was the dignity of work – regardless of who does it. So as I began dealing with these men who were building the Arch, I had tremendous respect for their ability and dedication, and pride in what they were doing. They knew they were building something unique. It had never been done before. They knew it was going to be "monumental." They knew it was going to be lasting. They knew it was going to be symbolic. They knew that people were going to look at it every day. They knew that it would be an achievement, and they were part of it. And I wanted to capture that. That's number one. And also I wanted to get a sense of challenge. I wanted to tell a story. There was an unknown – I mean, you can carry this a little too far, but it commemorates the chance-takers. The people who were going to move West. They didn't know what was going to be there, it was the unknown. So I wanted to tell this business of struggling for an unknown thing. I had that whole thing about skill and process, and then the historical overlay. So that's why there are references in the film to Lewis and Clark, references to the seasons, about moving through a period of time, and all of that.

We were shooting 16mm color reversal, not color negative. There was no 16mm color negative then. We kept losing cameramen. The cameramen I liked the best, the ones that I had worked most closely with on other pictures, and who I thought were the most skillful, began to request being taken off the job when we reached about 150 to 200 feet. They didn't like the heights. And by a stroke of luck there was one guy who I never thought was all that creative, but the guy was fearless. And he became invaluable, absolutely invaluable. He would go anywhere up there. He had no fear of heights at all.

When you went down there, the size of everything was just overwhelming. These huge pieces of metal. And then this thing going up, and we have to capture it on film. I realized that size is relative, and made sure that there were people in each of the shots we used, to give scale. I was concerned about myself – I didn't know how I was, in a sense, going to direct the thing, because you get up there and get petrified. But when my mind was on the job, the heights seemed to disappear. Except one time; we'd been working all day. I think we were at about 500 feet at that time, and we'd worked fairly late, and it was overcast and getting dark. We were coming down the ladder with our equipment. And the wind came up, maybe a 25-mile an hour wind. And the thing began to move. I was totally paralyzed. Just paralyzed. It's so funny. Why you think you can hold on tighter, and it will help you. Finally somebody moved, and then I moved, and we got down. That was the only time that I really got paralyzed.

SWAYING WITHOUT A NET
Fred Morris,
Ironworker on the Arch Project

The safety record on the Gateway Arch project was exemplary. Although insurance companies had come up with a figure estimating a possible 13 deaths during construction of the unique structure, there were no fatalities and no major injuries. On March 31, 1965, proud workers and managers gathered to commemorate 100 days of work without a lost time accident.

ONE problem with working on the Arch was the swaying. Once the Arch got up to about 500 feet, it was really swaying. One day a supervisor asked me how much I thought it was swaying, and I said, "two or three feet." "Oh," he said, "maybe one-tenth of that, it's not swaying nearly as much as that." They had instruments on it. Within a few days of that we hit some very high winds, 80 miles an hour plus, and this thing was really rocking. You couldn't weld. You couldn't hold an arc, and I am looking at the other leg over there and this thing is completely passing each other. And I told the guy I was working with, "Let's get the hell off of here." And about then the supervisor came down the steps, and he said, "Hey, get off." And I asked him, "Hey, how much is it swinging now?" He says, "Everything you think it is; this thing is really rolling, man." So we went down and you could actually look up and see it when you got back away from it. Everybody went down to a little tavern on Second Street and you could look up and see the booms moving on the derricks.

I know when we got up closer to the top, for whatever reason, they hung a net from one leg to another. There was a guy I worked with in our crew who was really crazy. The net was probably 50 feet below the top and he was telling me one day, "if you and I jumped off here into that net, they would have to come and get us with a derrick." And I said, "You would never hit the net, there is no way you could jump off there and hit that net." The wind was too strong when you got 600 feet in the air down by that river. We had an argument about it, and so on a Sunday we were working down there, and we took a large tow sack and we put into it what we thought was the same weight as this guy, we picked him up, then picked the sack up, until we said it was about the same weight. And there was nobody down there except us. And so we threw it off the Arch toward the net, but it missed the net and it came close to hitting the river.

6 DAYS WITHOUT AN ACCIDENT.
WE HAVE WORKED 100 CONSECUTIVE DAYS WITHOUT A LOST TIME ACCIDENT.
OUR RECORD IS 516 CONSECUTIVE DAYS WITHOUT A LOST TIME ACCIDENT.
LET'S BEAT THAT RECORD...

The safety record belied the constant danger inherent in the job. Bear in mind that the images you see on this page of workmen going about their jobs at over 600 feet above the ground also show men working without safety harnesses, who could depend only on themselves, their experience and sure-footedness to survive on a constantly moving structure composed of slick stainless steel. Men not only kept their balance but labored with wrenches, spanners, welding torches, mallets and other tools under these dizzying circumstances.

WRITING THE ARCH
Sue Ann Wood,
Journalist for the *St. Louis Globe-Democrat*

WRITING about the construction of the Gateway Arch was a principal, and favorite, assignment of mine as a young reporter for the *St. Louis Globe-Democrat* during the two and a half years that two giant columns of steel rose slowly above the downtown skyline, bending toward an eventual meeting point 630 feet above the ground.

I had asked for the assignment after the retirement of the *Globe* staff writer who had written most of the stories about the riverfront memorial and preparations for its construction. When the city editor granted my request, I hurried down to the National Park Service headquarters in the Old Courthouse to introduce myself to the memorial superintendent, LeRoy Brown. He and the man in charge of public relations, Gus Budde, happily agreed to keep me informed about every stage of the above-ground Arch construction that was about to begin.

Thus it was that I went with a photographer on a wintry morning, with snowflakes blowing in the air, to watch as the first huge triangle of steel was lifted by crane onto the base of what would be the south leg of the Arch. No other media people were there, so the *Globe-Democrat* had the only story and picture of that historic start of the great construction project.

I thought about that as I stood near the same spot on the riverfront on a bright October morning in 1965, surrounded by thousands of others gazing up at the sky. We were waiting to see the final segment of the Arch set in place between the two legs, now braced apart by a jack that kept the ends from touching.

Plenty of media representatives were there to witness this historic moment. Reporters and photographers were everywhere, on the ground and in the air, in hovering helicopters.

As I gazed up at the workers atop the Arch, moving around the heavy cranes that had lifted each steel section into place, I was remembering what I could certainly call my peak reporting experience.

I had come to the riverfront to get information for a big story on how the final steel triangle would be set in place, and was talking to Ted Rennison, one of the construction supervisors.

"I could explain it better if we were up there," he said, gesturing toward the Arch top. "Do you want to go up?"

(Bottom) Reporter Sue Ann Wood poses with Ted Rennison the day before their climb to the top of the Arch. The following day, Wood and Rennison posed atop the Arch (top) and had their photo taken from the opposite leg of the structure.

(Opposite page) A reading is taken directly beneath the soaring, nearly completed Arch in the summer of 1965.

I gulped and said, "Sure." He looked at the dress and high-heeled pumps I was wearing and suggested I come back the next day wearing pants and rubber-soled shoes, "because it's a little slippery up there."

So the next morning I arrived in jeans and sneakers, with a photographer. We were fitted with hard hats and went into the underground lobby area. There we took a work elevator part-way up the north leg, climbed stairs into what would later be the observation-deck area, up a wooden ladder through an open trap door and out onto a wide expanse of steel.

Although it was a hazy morning, the view for miles in every direction was breathtaking. A photograph that was taken of me atop the Arch is now on the wall over my computer, and I still get a tremor down my spine when I look at it and remember the thrill of being there.

Down in one misty corner of the photo can be seen a building under construction, the first of three apartment towers of the Mansion House complex being built near the riverfront. I had already reserved an apartment in that building, where I would live for nearly 30 years, with a view of the Mississippi River and the Gateway Arch that I never tired of seeing.

I cherish memories of the tiny role I was able to play in the building of one of the world's great monuments by reporting on each phase of its rise on the St. Louis riverfront, from the moment on a wintry day when that first huge triangle of steel was set in place.

(Right) Crane operators on the Arch project included (left to right) Jerry Contrell, Jim Pearl, north derrick operator Bill Quigley (and top), south derrick operator Luther Fritts, and Leo Covington.

(Bottom) One of the most difficult lifts made during the construction of the Arch was this one, when the stabilizing strut was positioned between the legs of the Arch at the 530-foot level. The 255-foot long strut weighed 60 tons, and had to be lifted simultaneously by the two operators, in their shacks on the ground, directed by one man at the top.

(Opposite page) Luther Fritts is shown here at the controls of the south derrick. Operators lifted sections into place, and also loaded pieces of the interior infrastructure through the top, delivered welding materials and other tools, lowered waste from the port-a-johns, and acted as the major evacuation route for any seriously injured workmen - a role which they fortunately did not have to play.

COMPLETING THE ARCH
Bill Quigley,
Crane Operator, PDM

I was sent down to the Arch from our local union hall to run the derrick on the north leg in 1963. If I remember right, the north leg was at 60 feet or thereabouts, and the south leg derrick had already been erected; they were just putting the derrick on the north leg. The south leg derrick was operated by Luther Fritts. He was 72 years old when he came down there, but he was more like a guy of 23. He was a very personable guy, smoked 100 cigars a week. I remember one of the bosses saying, "I don't know what they sent that old guy down here for." But two days later he was saying, "Is there some way we can slow that old guy down?"

Each individual leg had its own operator. Both sides were not doing the same thing all the time. Some of them were welding, some were putting braces in, and some were maybe a day or two ahead of time, as far as getting ready to make another lift. So the only logical way to do it was to have a crane on each side that would handle each task in its turn. A lot of people think that the creeper crane was a new idea, but it really wasn't. It was

new to St. Louis, but in New York and even Chicago, those methods were used for quite a long time. The derrick was really a standard derrick.

The hoists were sitting 100 feet behind each leg on the ground. The shed had cables running up to the derrick on top, to the pulleys on the track, and the phone links running down for the signalman to

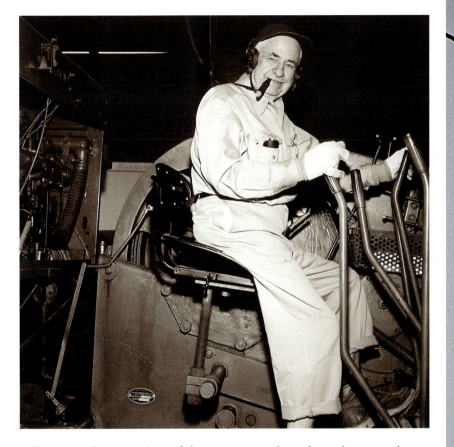

talk to us. The operation of the cranes was done from the ground. The hoist was on the ground, and so was I, the operator. The big thing was to keep weight off of the Arch itself. If I remember right, I think that the derricks weighed about 70 to 80 tons. So the hoist cable went down to a shack at the bottom of the Arch, and everything was done by telephone. I would wear earphones, and there would be a man up on top, directing the procedure by talking to you. And it was really not much different than you talking to your neighbor, or your relatives, only he'd be telling you two or three things to do at one time. The cable itself was the longest that I ever worked with. The load line for the main load was 5,600 feet. It came back and was handled on two drums and a hoist, which is really not a normal procedure. There is not often a call for that high a lift, or that much cable.

The sections of the Arch, as most everybody called them, were known to us as "cans." The vernacular on the job was that "there was going to be another can set." And when they'd bring another can up, as the Arch went up higher, the can got a little bit smaller in width, size, and weight. After I'd set it down, they'd weld it, and then they'd have to put their rebars in it for the concrete, just like they do on a bridge. They also used post-tensioning bars that they had to stretch out at different stations.

(Left) With the assistance of a crane operator, a section is shown being positioned for assembly welding.

(Right) As the project neared the top, it became more difficult for the signalman at the top to see the construction site.

(Opposite page) The creeper derricks are seen silhouetted against the evening sky in this view, taken during the summer of 1965.

A lot of people think because the operator sits on the ground and you can't see what you are doing, that it takes a lot longer, and you are not as precise. But to people that have been around that type of work, it works very, very, well. Especially when you have some good people that are doing signaling on the phone, that gives you a mental picture. The ironworkers that we had down there were extremely good, and very clear in the picture that they would give you.

One of the things that happened to me, and that I really respect, is that I have four fingers missing on my right hand, and the two derrick operators had to take physicals, and Pittsburgh-Des Moines' insurance company turned me down to run the derrick. Which I thought was unfair, but what I really appreciated was that the people that worked there, the ironworkers, their officers, and the officers of our union, all went to bat for me, and with that the company decided that I ought to at least have a chance. And I was very proud of that. When you lift a section, the men up there have to trust the guy that's running the crane, because, if something happens, there aren't too many places to run. A comfortable feeling goes a long way up there.

The crew that was down there was a combination of a lot of personalities. But by chance it happened that the personalities all went together, and everybody had a good time. It was a fun place to work. I can't ever remember an argument in the 33 months I was down there.

On the day of the setting of the last piece, they had boats in the river blowing whistles. The mayor. Just hundreds, thousands of people downtown watching what was going on. I don't think there was much work being done in the buildings downtown, because everybody was at a window. The only bad part about me putting the last can in place was that I'm the only guy that didn't see it until the film came out!

(Opposite page, top left and right) As the Arch neared its completion, it gave stronger and stronger hints of the irreplaceable icon it was to become, dominating the St. Louis skyline with its graceful, though unfinished curve. The stabilizing strut was necessary to take stress off the legs and their post-tensioning bars; when the strut was placed, at the 530-foot level, the Arch legs were each leaning inward 150 feet off center.

(Opposite page, bottom left) The sleek, streamlined Admiral excursion boat, completed in 1940, passes by the Arch. A favorite city attraction, it made river cruises between 1940 and 1979. The boat was converted into a stationary dockside casino in 1998. It is 375 feet long, with five decks and a 4,400-passenger capacity.

(Left and middle) As the massive legs of the Arch moved closer together, they reached a point where the special "collar" scaffolding had to be removed, and the gap narrowed so far that boards were placed from north to south and workmen could cross between the structures. Moving and removing materials at this stage of construction remained an intricate procedure.

(Right) Vito Comparato (left, sitting on rail) was the signalman on the north leg, and worked with derrick operator Bill Quigley by telephone hookup.

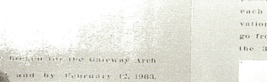

A system of eight cars, carrying five passengers per car will traverse each leg of the Arch to an observation deck. An elevator will also go from the Visitor Center area to the 372-foot level.

(Opposite page) St. Louis dignitaries including (seated, left to right) former mayor Bernard Dickmann, then-mayor Alfonso Cervantes, and former mayor Raymond Tucker signed their names to a "signatorium sheet" in a special ceremony at the Old St. Louis Post Office.

(Top) Workmen and others added their signatures as objects were placed in the time capsule on October 27, 1965.

(Bottom) With the capsule sealed and ready to go, workmen slipped it in between the inner and outer skins of the last Arch section on the evening before the completion of the Arch.

Two time capsules were placed in and near the Gateway Arch in 1965. The first time capsule was buried near the south leg of the Arch on January 19, 1965. It was described in a local newspaper as a "craftsman's capsule," and contained "printing memorabilia of the city."

The second time capsule was placed in the final section of the Arch on October 27, 1965, between the outer skin of stainless steel and the inner carbon steel skin. Photographs were taken of the time capsule being seated in between the walls of the section while the piece was still on the ground. Area school children were encouraged to sign their names to lists that were enclosed in the capsule. A total of 762,000 people signed the "signatorium sheets." The capsule also contained area newspapers. No date was set for the capsule to be opened in 1965. In fact, its position within the final section made it impossible to retrieve as long as the Arch stands, for on October 28, 1965, the final triangular section of the Arch was hoisted into place and welded together with the rest of the structure. The Arch would literally have to be taken apart to gain access to this time capsule.

In the days leading up to October 27, 1965, the scaffolding had been removed from the top of the Arch, and a narrow sliver of just 2 feet separated the legs.

(Opposite page) The great moment would come on October 28, when it would be discovered if the final section would fit and if the completed Arch would stand on its own.

THE DAY THE ARCH WAS FINISHED

The big day, Thursday, October 28, 1965, finally arrived. On this day the final of the 142 sections of the Gateway Arch was to be set in place. Squeezed into place might be a more apt description. The two gigantic 630-foot tall legs which the final section would join and make into an Arch were leaning toward one another with tremendous weight and force, held back only by post-tensioned steel and the stabilizing strut; they stood just 2 feet apart. Into this gap an 8-foot wide section, measuring 17 feet on each of the three exposed sides and weighing 10 tons, would have to be inserted. Huge jacks would be used to exert 500 tons of pressure to open the gap to 8 $\frac{1}{2}$ feet.

Although a ceremony had been scheduled for 10 a.m., engineers and workers were worried. They knew that the heat of the sun shining on the south leg would begin a subtle expansion of the metal, elongating it by as much as 11 inches in a short period and skewing it so that wedding north leg to south leg would be impossible until the metal cooled once more. In fact, the engineers advocated "closing" the Arch at night, an idea that was quickly vetoed by politicians and civic boosters. The engineers and workers conceded a daytime ceremony, but proceeded at 9:25 a.m. instead of 10 a.m. to hoist the last section. The lift took 13 minutes. To counteract the south leg's expansion from the sun's heat, the St. Louis Fire Department used 700 feet of hose to spray cold water 550 feet up the south leg, continuing from 9:30 a.m. until the end of the operation. As the final section rose into the air the crowds cheered, steam whistles on riverboats were blown, and the city rejoiced. Some school children watched the event on television, while other classes and scout groups were on site. Work in neighboring buildings came to a halt as all eyes turned toward the Arch.

Among the guests were Luther Ely Smith, Jr., son of the park's founder, and Bernard Dickmann, the politician who did so much to make the project a reality in the 1930s. The then-mayor, Alfonso Cervantes, took center stage along with Eero Saarinen's widow Aline, an arts correspondent for NBC's "Today" show. Undersecretary of the Interior John A. Carver, Jr., spoke and Superintendent LeRoy Brown served as master of ceremonies, while Vice President Hubert Humphrey viewed the proceedings from an overhead airplane. After the last piece was jockeyed into position at 11:04 a.m. the delicate job was almost over. In the afternoon, at 2 p.m., workers released the 12-ton bottle jacks and the full weight of the two legs secured the final section. The stainless steel did not buckle. Welding remained the final chore, and took up two days of work. Superintendent Brown exclaimed to his co-workers, "No other comparable event is likely to occur in our lifetime."

But despite the fact that the final piece had been set the work was not yet over. Even though all the attention had been, up to then, focused on the completion of the Arch, there was still much to be done.

The final piece, outfitted with an American flag, stands ready to be hoisted into place, completing the structure of the Gateway Arch. The last section had special beams built into the outer edges of it, following the triangular shape, as well as locating holes in the corners which would match five-inch locating pins.

(Opposite page) St. Louis held its breath as the final piece was hauled skyward. Huge crowds on land beneath the Arch, on the river in boats, in the windows and rooftops of downtown buildings, and on television in their homes, watched the dramatic moment.

In these views, the widened gap at the top can be seen, forced apart by the action of huge jacks and a loosening of the bolts on the stabilizing strut. Heavy members were built into the adjacent sections to support the beams that performed the "pushing." These had hydraulic cylinders on them, and when the pumps were started they could exert up to 700 tons of pressure; they used 500 tons to push the Arch sections back a total of 6 feet. Safety bars were placed so that the positioning of the Arch legs could be controlled at all times. The heat of the sun on the south leg of the Arch caused it to elongate. To combat this, the raising of the final section was set for early in the morning, and the St. Louis Fire Department did their part by cooling the south leg with a fire hose, minimizing the distortion.

114

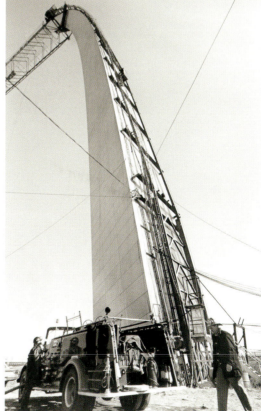

*The moment of triumph is marked by workmen
standing atop the final piece. It took about three
hours to fit and secure the final section in place.*

Jubilant workers gathered around the American flag at the top of construction, 630 feet above the ground. Over two and a half years of hard work culminated in the completion of the triumphal structure, which true to the predictions of the Severud firm, was structurally sound.

A NEW VISION

While workmen continued to secure the final section, speeches and congratulations were made far below. Aline Saarinen, second wife of the architect and a well-known art and architecture commentator for NBC News, was a featured speaker at the ceremony.

117

CHAPTER 7
THE RIVERFRONT MEMORIAL

1966-1985

The completion of the Gateway Arch's structure on October 28, 1965 was by far not the end of the story of the memorial. The park was a long way from being able to throw open the doors and let visitors start pouring in. A visitor center, a heating and air conditioning system, a working tram to the top, landscaping, and a museum were some of the larger projects which still awaited completion. Just moving the creeper derricks down the legs, putting in plugs of stainless steel where holes had been made to support the derrick tracks and polishing the structure, took nearly a year. During that time the interior of the structure was finished, including final installation of the tram capsules, emergency stairways, ductwork, electrical work, and other necessities. Meanwhile the underground visitor center was completed and opened to the public with some temporary exhibits on June 9, 1967. Over a month later, on July 24, 1967, nearly two years after the completion of the Arch structure, the north tram inaugurated operations, taking the first visitors from the general public to the top. The south tram began service over six months later, on March 19, 1968. Finally, on May 25, 1968, in an official ceremony, Vice President Hubert Humphrey dedicated the Gateway Arch. Because of a severe rainstorm, the ceremony was held in the underground visitor center; malfunctioning drains at the entrance ramps allowed water to flood the building to a depth of several inches. Later projects included the museum and the landscaping.

Washing, buffing, disguising holes from the creeper derrick tracks, and other cosmetic activities took place during late 1965 and into 1966. The creeper derricks were slowly lowered to ground level and removed, with track being taken off as they moved downward.

Inside the Arch, the trams were installed and cosmetic changes were made, especially in building the observation deck at the top of the Arch, which included a platform to stand on and an attractive viewing area with windows. The rails for the tram were raised from the inside at the bottom, a section at a time, and bolted into place in the Arch. One section of rails in the lower load zone on each side was left out temporarily so that the individual capsules could be put in one at a time, as well as the counterweights and tensioning weights.

(Opposite page) The monumental Eads Bridge, an engineering marvel of 1874, flanks the completed Gateway Arch, a marvel of equal importance of 1965. The creeper derricks are nearing the base of the Arch in this photo, taken in April 1966.

The landscaping of the Arch grounds was completed in phases between 1971 and 1980. The original grassy fields on a flat plain, evident when the Arch was just completed (bottom) were augmented by the curvilinear walks designed by Saarinen and the rolling hills and valleys created by Kiley (top).

(Opposite page) By 1990, the forest envisioned by Dan Kiley during the competition in 1947, with the Arch rising above it, had come to be, although the number of trees was reduced and the dominant species had been changed by the National Park Service from tulip poplar to Rosehill ash. Despite the many changes to his landscape, Kiley was very pleased with the look of the landscape during site visits in the 1990s.

dominant species in 1971, when the landscaping of the site was begun. The loose groupings of shade trees and curvilinear ponds that visitors see at JNEM are not typical of Kiley's work. In preceding projects, independent elements float to some degree, lacking the coherency of JNEM and subsequent schemes, but never in the guise of the romantic style of landscape design. In his first built works, completed while employed by Warren Manning, Kiley's informality stemmed from Manning's interest in

horticultural display over site structure. In larger plans, such as the Willow Run and Lily Pond housing projects (1942), under the direction of Louis Kahn, Kiley's landscapes were pared down to straightforward extensions and reiterations of circulation and architectural lines. By the early 1950s, Kiley was increasingly adept at manipulating formal elements both in relation to specific architectural anchors, as found in the site plans of the Hollin Hills development (1953) and more strongly at Currier Farm (1959), and as infrastructure within larger sites, as in the Concordia campus plan (1955) and the Detroit Civic Center (1955). Open space was increasingly defined by its proportional relationship to adjacent forms and often by a geometrically defined ground plane.

Three words summarize the pivotal role played by JNEM in an emerging landscape architect's career: "Get Dan Kiley." With these words, Kiley recalled in interviews, Eero Saarinen encouraged his colleagues in the burgeoning postwar architectural field to hire the young landscape designer. Without the Saarinen connection and the publicity of JNEM, Kiley's practice would have taken much longer to establish itself. These words also make reference to something that is more difficult to describe. By selecting Kiley as the landscape architect of choice for prominent competitions such as Quito, Ecuador (1944) and JNEM, Saarinen joined Louis Kahn, Oscar Stonorov, Minoru Yamasaki, Chuck Goodwin, Skidmore, Owings and Merrill, I.M. Pei, Harry Weese and other leading voices in American

modernist architecture in proposing that Dan Kiley's vision of strong,
functional form and fluid spatial interplay could be the landscape equiva-
lent of their structural work, nothing less than a prototype for the modern
American landscape. With Dan Kiley, projects such as JNEM suggested
that one could understand the dynamic, formal landscape freed from the
legacy of Frederick Law Olmsted and the strictures of Beaux-Arts formulas.

A MUSEUM TO TELL THE STORY

Aram Mardirosian,
Architect, Designer of the
Museum of Westward Expansion

(Bottom) The dedication of the Museum of Westward Expansion took place on August 23, 1976. Attendees included (left to right) National Park Service Director Gary Everhardt, museum designer Aram Mardirosian, and JNEM Maintenance Supervisor Ted Rennison.

(Top) The statue of Thomas Jefferson stands at the entrance to the museum, symbolizing Jefferson's role in expanding the nation through the Louisiana Purchase and sending Lewis and Clark westward.

DESIGNING the Museum of Westward Expansion was a search for an answer to the critical question: How can a museum be a meaningful part of the Jefferson National Expansion Memorial?

Located in the historic waterfront district of St. Louis, itself a significant part of the history of America's westward expansion, the Gateway Arch is an evocative and graceful form for a memorial commemorating the country's expansion following the Louisiana Purchase by Thomas Jefferson in 1803 and concluding in 1890, the date identified by the historian Frederick Jackson Turner as the time when America's frontiers were closed.

The story of that expansion is as immense in scope as it is varied in its details. Beyond the innumerable facts which can be agreed upon, the experience of those directly involved in the story itself often varies significantly – be they explorers or mountain men, miners seeking their fortunes or soldiers sent west to show the flag, Native Americans trying to preserve their ancient way of life or settlers trying to establish a new life in America. The challenge was to develop an inclusive design concept that would embrace a larger view of history – what had preceded and what would follow this extraordinary period of America's history both within the country and in the world as a whole – while focusing upon those telling "bits and pieces" of history

that remain from these individual experiences and combine to tell the overall story of what happened, where it happened, and who was involved. This approach also minimizes interpretive structures by using firsthand accounts, the actual words of the participants themselves, as well as the available physical evidence of their lives – their shoes, their tools, their clothing – as evocations of the real stories of those sometimes famous but most often anonymous lives which did so much to shape our country.

Carved from the vast underground space beneath the Gateway Arch, the museum's circular design of expanding rings seeks to create a space-time continuum to provide an appropriate three-dimensional, multisensory visitor experience using a hierarchy of chronologically organized documentary materials relating to the history, natural history, technology, art and music of the American West. The exhibit encourages visitors to share in this historical experience and to perceive changes in our view of ourselves and of history through time. The focal point at the center of the circle at 1803 is the starting point in time of the story, the year when Thomas Jefferson was president, the Louisiana Territory was purchased from France, and Lewis and Clark were asked by Jefferson to undertake their historic journey of discovery.

(Top left) National Park Service Director George B. Hartzog, Jr. (left) is one of many interested auditors of Aram Mardirosian's concept for the Museum of Westward Expansion at a presentation held in 1971. Concepts included an open plan to allow easy visitor access and egress, and a chronological set of "time rings" to enable visitors to understand the scope and depth of a century of westward expansion.

(Top right) Artifacts include items made and used by American Indians of several tribal groups. Footwear, an extremely personal and representational item in any culture, is used throughout the museum to accentuate cultural ties and differences.

(Bottom) Aram Mardirosian's vision for the Museum of Westward Expansion is dramatically expressed in this vignette, which juxtaposes an 18th-century Spanish carreta with a photograph of Earth from space. Carretas were used in the Southwest until at least the 1830s; men landed on the moon less than 140 years later. Thus, with two dramatic artifacts, Mardirosian was able to convey the scope of the period encapsulated in the museum.

The concept of time and space gives us the means by which we are able to locate ourselves and determine how far we have traveled and the changes we have experienced. The space-time context was developed with the thought that it could provide an appropriate, provocative and informative way for visitors to view the vastness and complexity of history; and for children, parents, teachers and others to use the museum and its resources to explore, discuss and interpret the seemingly infinite scope and complexity of the story.

Designing the museum, however, was only a part of the story of how the Museum of Westward Expansion came to be what it is today. There would certainly not be a museum of the scale and scope of what was built without the decision by George B. Hartzog, Jr. to have an appropriate museum as an integral part of the memorial design. Nor would the museum have the extraordinarily high level of integration with the structure without the efforts of Frank Phillips, who retired as head of exhibit and museum construction for the National Park Service to come to St. Louis to supervise and implement the construction.

THE DEDICATION OF THE GATEWAY ARCH

(Left) A boy sloshed through the standing water inside the Arch visitor center on the day of the dedication.

(Right) Principal speakers posed outside the Arch in the rain, (left to right) Vice President Hubert Humphrey, Secretary of the Interior Stewart Udall, Missouri Governor Warren Hearnes and St. Louis Mayor Alfonso Cevantes.

(Opposite page) The unveiling of the dedication plaque by Vice President Humphrey.

The dedication of the Gateway Arch was more memorable perhaps for the unbelievably bad weather than for any other single aspect of the ceremony. The dedication was held on May 25, 1968, nearly three years after the completion of the Arch. In many ways the dedication ceremony was a mere formality, because the complex had been open to the public for over a year. Trams began taking visitors to the top when the north tram began operations on July 24, 1967, and the south tram was opened on March 19, 1968. The dedication was supposed to take place in a grand outdoor ceremony, to be held on the grounds beneath the Arch with bands and speeches, but the day of the dedication began with a light rain at about 7 a.m. which grew steadily worse. The decision to move the event inside was made at 10:00 a.m., and rainfall was measured at 2.41 inches by noon.

Vice President Hubert H. Humphrey was the principal speaker; President Lyndon B. Johnson had been invited but declined. Johnson had stated that he would not seek nor accept his party's nomination for another term as president, which left the Democratic candidacy for the office wide open. The dedication of the Arch was held in a time of political turmoil, less than two months after the assassination of Martin Luther King, Jr. on April 4 and two weeks prior to the assassination of Robert F. Kennedy on June 6, 1968, so security was tight.

The program was devised by Conrad Heine, a National Park Service employee and historian from Washington, D.C., whose job it was to plan and execute dedication ceremonies. Due to the Park

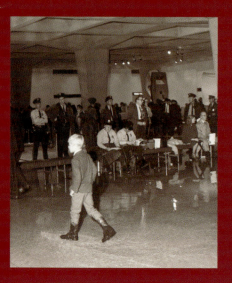

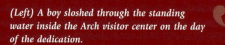

Honored Guest Ticket

The Dedication of the Gateway Arch
SAINT LOUIS, MISSOURI

Saturday, May 25, 1968 - 11:00 A.M.

ADMIT ONE

The Secretary of the Interior
The Chairman
of
The United States Territorial
Expansion Memorial Commission
and
The Mayor of Saint Louis
request
the honor of your presence
at the
Dedication of
The Gateway Arch
at
eleven o'clock in the morning
Saturday, the Twenty-fifth of May
Nineteen Hundred and Sixty-eight
at
The Jefferson National Expansion Memorial
Saint Louis, Missouri

R.s.v.p.
National Park Service
11 North Fourth Street
Saint Louis, Missouri 63102

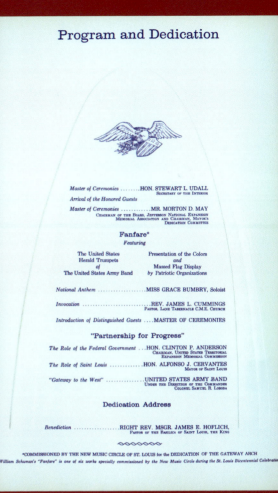

Service's "Mission 66 Program," scores of visitor centers and other facilities were being opened and dedicated at the time. A large number of tickets, some 10,000, were printed, a grand and elaborate program was planned, and a special fanfare was written for the event. Teams of rangers were brought in from all sections of the country, and coordination with local law enforcement was flawless. In all of the planning, however, no provision was made for rain. Assistant Superintendent Harry Pfanz recalled, "It was decided that it would not rain, it would be a clear day. I don't know whether this came from Washington or where, but it would be a clear day. Don't plan any alternatives." Pfanz arrived that morning amid one of the fiercest downpours anyone had ever seen in St. Louis, and, he continued, "I couldn't get any answers. They wouldn't cancel it. So we got as many chairs as we could from outside and set them up in the lobby, around the fountain. A large freestanding mural was on the west side of the fountain, so a lectern

was placed there, and the chairs were placed around the other three sides. Then they started moving television equipment in there. We had people in the top of the Arch, Secret Service men, FBI and police, to watch for snipers."

Finally, at 11 a.m., the crowds were allowed to come in, dripping wet. There was a much smaller turnout than expected, but the visitor center became very crowded all the same. Vice President Humphrey began to speak, but, Pfanz related: "All of sudden, the water came pouring down the ramps. They had drains across the ramps to catch normal flow, but it was raining so hard that it was running right over the drains, and came into the visitor center, among all of those electrical cables. Well, at some point one of the people sitting in the crowd, some protestor, stood up and shouted something, and someone sitting behind him swatted him. The Secret Service took him off."

The interior of the visitor center was flooded with over an inch of standing water, and people left the brief ceremony with soggy shoes to be drenched once again as they made their way home in the rain.

CHAPTER 8

ICON IN THE CITY

1986-2005

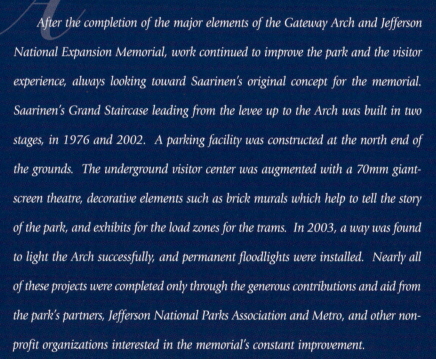

*A*fter the completion of the major elements of the Gateway Arch and Jefferson National Expansion Memorial, work continued to improve the park and the visitor experience, always looking toward Saarinen's original concept for the memorial. Saarinen's Grand Staircase leading from the levee up to the Arch was built in two stages, in 1976 and 2002. A parking facility was constructed at the north end of the grounds. The underground visitor center was augmented with a 70mm giant-screen theatre, decorative elements such as brick murals which help to tell the story of the park, and exhibits for the load zones for the trams. In 2003, a way was found to light the Arch successfully, and permanent floodlights were installed. Nearly all of these projects were completed only through the generous contributions and aid from the park's partners, Jefferson National Parks Association and Metro, and other non-profit organizations interested in the memorial's constant improvement.

The level of interest from organizations and individuals has remained high because the Gateway Arch has become such a vital part of the life of the community. Not only is it the undisputed icon of the city of St. Louis, but it now permeates the lives and memories of every St. Louis resident to the point where the St. Louis living experience is inseparable from some connection with the Arch.

The construction of the Gateway Arch also led to the renaissance of Downtown St. Louis for which Luther Ely Smith and the other founders had hoped. In conjunction with Busch Stadium, which was built at the same time, the Arch promised an influx of people and interest in downtown which continues to grow. Corporate headquarters for the Pet Corporation, Sverdrup Engineering, Ralston Purina, and other firms were set up in brand-new buildings, while hotels, restaurants, office buildings, parking garage complexes, a convention center, a new arena, a domed football stadium, and other structures also sprouted on the St. Louis skyline. Older buildings like the Fur Exchange, the Cupples Warehouses, the Wainwright Building, the Old Post Office, St. Louis Union Station, structures in the Laclede's Landing District, and the "loft district" along Washington Avenue were rehabbed. The Arch drew St. Louis' major-league sports teams in baseball, football and hockey to play in the downtown area, ensuring a perpetual influx of fan-based tourism and consumption.

The future will bring an even closer relationship between the Arch and the city, as the park administration reaches out to embrace civic leaders and partnerships, and as a physical connection is contemplated which will link city and park across the void of the Interstate Highway and Memorial Drive on the park's west side. Exciting times lie ahead for the Gateway Arch, the "giant striding into the future."

THE ARCH AND REDEVELOPMENT
Eric Sandweiss,
Indiana University

THE Jefferson National Expansion Memorial germinated as a plan to save the St. Louis waterfront long before it took the form, or acquired the commemorative justification, that it did in the 1930s and 1940s. To understand the Arch, you need to understand as much about St. Louis real estate and city planning practice as you do the history of the Louisiana Purchase or of the travels of Lewis and Clark.

The connection dates back at least to the 1890s, when St. Louis business and political leaders began to consider the benefits of a comprehensive public-private approach to the challenge of maintaining their city's prosperity. Their search for a means to realize that approach dovetailed nicely with the burgeoning profession of city planning, which merged landscape design, engineering, social work, and fiscal policy into a persuasive and potentially powerful program for ordering the notoriously unpredictable process of urban growth.

From as early as the publication of the St. Louis Civic League's 1907 "Plan for St. Louis," which laid out the city planners' agenda for the dawning century, prominent local businesspeople and social reformers focused a good portion of their concern on the blocks that would soon be labeled "The Central Waterfront." Here, on the slope that led up from the Mississippi's west bank to a ridge line corresponding to today's Fourth Street, Pierre Laclede had in 1764 platted a simple grid of some two dozen blocks that held the commercial, residential, and administrative needs of his trading outpost.

The problem with this well-laid plan, of course, was that the trading post turned into a city that quickly outgrew its snug confines by the river bank. As St. Louis grew in size, its central riverfront went from being the symbolic and civic heart of the city to becoming an ill-used adjunct to a burgeoning downtown district. East of Fourth Street, the city looked quite different. Difficult to access, hemmed in by railroad tracks and the Eads Bridge, the original blocks of the village saw virtually no new development after the 1870s.

And so it was that the authors of the "Plan for St. Louis" settled on the idea of sacrificing the city's historic heart for a statement about its future. In place of the central waterfront as it then existed, they projected a monumental and largely ceremonial gateway. By the time city officials succeeded in drawing in federal funds on the promise of a national monument to westward expansion, the plan for reviving property values in the city's heart was nearly three decades old.

The eventual redevelopment strategy that emerged for downtown made the Arch grounds a distinct tourist destination, separated from downtown by a depressed highway speeding motorists through the city's heart. To their west, the Civic Center Redevelopment Corporation would take advantage of urban renewal-era

innovations allowing designated groups to acquire privately held land for the public good; their acquisitions resulted in the clearing of a remnant of the city's Chinatown for Busch Memorial Stadium and surrounding parking facilities. Together, the stadium, the preserved Courthouse, and the Arch created a foundation of tourist landmarks on which rested the revival of downtown commercial construction that transformed the St. Louis skyline from the 1970s through the 1990s.

The Arch did not save downtown St. Louis. New construction and historic preservation both had a momentum of their own, with or without the Jefferson National Expansion Memorial. But in its boldness, its recognizability, and its embrace of open space in what had been St. Louis' most crowded blocks, the memorial announced a new approach to using and maintaining the city's heart. From the 1960s forward, tourism, recreation, and commemorative space would fill the void left by the inevitable passing of the functions that had shaped the distinctive historic downtown landscape.

In a photo taken not long after the completion of the Gateway Arch, large empty lots can be seen nearby. Within a few short years these areas had been filled in with high-rise office buildings, corporate headquarters, hotels, multilevel parking garages and Busch Stadium, originally used for both baseball and football sporting events.

135

The Gateway Arch, Busch Stadium, and the Stadium East Parking Garage are seen under simultaneous construction in the winter of 1965.

(Opposite page) This 2005 photo shows a revitalized downtown district, with a new stadium being constructed between the old one and the highway.

My Life with the Arch
Julius K. Hunter,
Vice President, Community Relations,
Saint Louis University

THE magnificent Gateway Arch and I have passed in and out of each other's lives frequently since its conception – and mine. I was just two years old when two St. Louis visionaries, James Ford and Luther Ely Smith passed the hat among their like-minded friends in 1945 and came up with the princely sum of $225,000 to spark entries for an appropriate memorial to St. Louis' key role in westward expansion. The winner was a giant stainless steel wicket of unprecedented design. I was heading out to kindergarten at Cole Elementary School when Eero Saarinen's unique design beat out all other competitors in 1948. The world might eventually thank Saarinen for scrapping his onetime musings about a concrete Arch and his early thoughts of having the legs straddle the Mississippi River.

When I learned the word "catenary" from the *Globe-Democrat* and *Post-Dispatch* accounts of the Arch plans, I used the dictionary that my fourth grade teacher, Miss Johnetta Jackson, had given me to lock the word in my mind. I just might be crowned champ in the unlikely event I were ever called on to lay out the precise order of the letters to c-a-t-e-n-a-r-y in a National Spelling Bee.

In 1961 – the year I graduated from Sumner High School – construction crewmen began digging to reach bedrock for the Arch's foundation. They found firm footing at an amazing 45 feet below ground level. As I entered my junior high school year, St. Louisans and curious tourists began seeing work underway above ground for the first time. I consumed and memorized other mind-boggling figures regarding the Arch. 630 feet tall. Legs spread 630 feet apart. An eventual 1,076 steps if one chose to trudge to the top. But elevator cars would be available almost to the top if one chose not to be courageous. 8 ½ million dollars worth of steel!

As I entered my senior year at Harris Teachers College the nefarious neighing of naysayers and demeaning din of detractors made even the most confident among us wonder if the two rising legs would actually come together as planned or whether a catastrophic miscalculation would cause a failed steel synapse. The fact that fourteen post-tensioning rods didn't do their job; that a major recalculation was ordered in the summer of 1964; that premature wrinkles developed on two of the massive pieces only added grist for the scathing skeptics to chew on.

As controversy bubbled over whether the Arch legs would be a hit or a miss, the eighth grade students I now taught at Hamilton Elementary

Arch maintenance employees change the aircraft warning light on the top of the Arch, an annual procedure (bottom), while in several other views, the Arch stands serenely fulfilling Luther Ely Smith's original dream of a fitting and aesthetically pleasing riverfront memorial.

School were among the thousands of local children invited to submit signature rolls and essays to be placed inside the Arch cap piece. We contributed with delight.

I got a wonderful two-week late twenty-second birthday present, when on October 28, 1965, a grand and glorious topping-out ceremony was held to celebrate the successful linking of the north and south legs.

But my life's intertwining with the birth and development of the Gateway Arch didn't stop there. In the spring of 1971, as an adventurous cub reporter, my Channel 5 TV crew and I poked our heads out of the hatch at the top of the Arch to film the annual changing of the 620-watt strobe aircraft warning light bulb. Then, in the earliest days of television news microwave coverage, I was a party to Channel 4's frequent unsanctioned bouncing of microwave signals off the Arch to bring our metro-area viewers "live" coverage. What's more, as a news anchor I reported for more than three decades on every zany, illegal, and tragic attempt to fly a plane through the Arch's legs or parachute to a landing atop it.

Hail to the Gateway Arch, an internationally acclaimed and personally appreciated landmark, that for me, as with so many others, has become an integral part of the story of our lives.

GROWING UP IN THE SHADOW OF THE ARCH
Tim Tucker,
Grandson of Mayor Raymond Tucker,
Downtown St. Louis Developer

MY love affair with the Arch started at the age of six. I remember riding in the back seat of my grandfather's car, driving down to the banks of the Mississippi River to check on the Arch's construction progress. I marveled at the engineering concept that these two independent stainless steel legs would eventually align and meet 630 feet in the air. As construction progressed I wondered along with everyone else if the last piece would fit! Eero Saarinen's inspirational sculpture is now internationally recognized as an icon of the city of St. Louis. When you first think of St. Louis you think of the Arch. St. Louis and the National Park Service constructed a simple, timeless structure that is as fresh today as it was the day it was completed.

As a planner and developer, having grown up in the shadow of the Arch, I have a deeper appreciation of the Arch's majesty and symbolism. To me the Arch represents the highest achievement in community cooperation, persistence, and optimism. The Arch embodies the ability of an incredibly diverse group of people to work together toward conceiving and implementing a seemingly impossible dream over a very long period of time without succumbing to major obstacles and losing focus. The Arch is an excellent example of the benefits that can be achieved by a community working together toward a common goal, rather than being

at odds with one another. The Arch provides as inspiration for cooperation and persistence.

The Arch is the focal point of downtown. It is also a mark in time that represents a dignified tribute to our past as the "Gateway to the West" and is a physical benchmark against which we can assess the quality of our future projects. The Arch represents stability in our urban evolution and continues to inspire development. The Arch has inspired billions of dollars of investment ranging from the construction of office buildings and their evolving conversions to residential condominiums, hotels, and apartments. The Arch is also indirectly responsible for the economic resurgence of East St. Louis.

I never grow tired of catching glimpses of the Arch from all around the city; it is a landmark, and if you can see it you have an idea of where you are. I love spying the Arch through buildings in the Central Business District, or the vertical views of the Arch from the North or the South. I especially like approaching the Arch from the south on Leonor K. Sullivan Boulevard, where the flood wall falls away, catching the Arch and Eads Bridge arches in the background. I enjoy running past the Arch all times of day or night in all weather conditions, watching the clouds and the ambient soft city lights, sunrises and sunsets reflecting off the stainless steel. I love to watch the rain, snow, insects, birds, and people swirl on and around its legs.

I am eternally grateful to all those men and women that contributed to the conception, implementation, and continuing management of the Arch. Imagine the void that would exist in St. Louis, the nation, and the world if the Arch was never built.

Visitors to the top of the Arch have included such well-known people as Dwight D. Eisenhower, Prince Charles of Great Britain, Lucille Ball, Robert Cummings, Lawrence Welk and his orchestra, Johnny Carson and Joseph Campanella. Visitors to the grounds have included Presidents Richard M. Nixon, Gerald R. Ford, Jimmy Carter, Ronald Reagan and George H.W. Bush.

During the 1990s the visitor center at Jefferson National Expansion Memorial achieved a cohesive design, and many new venues opened for visitors. These included revamped loading zones for the trams (bottom) which used exhibits to tell the story of the construction of the Arch and the historic 1850s St. Louis levee.

The park's original theater, named for Mayor Raymond R. Tucker, has shown the film "Monument to the Dream" since 1972. It received a new façade in 1997 by artist Jay Tschetter of Lincoln, Nebraska (top right) measuring 45 feet long and 15 feet tall, commemorating the men and women who made the Gateway Arch a reality. The façade of the Tucker Theater, like

that of the Odyssey Theatre on the south side of the visitor center, was created entirely of carved bricks. A scale model stainless steel Arch frames brick vignettes of the men and women who made the Arch a reality, with a full figure of architect Eero Saarinen at the very center. To each side of the Arch are famous landmarks and memorials in many regions of the United States, all carved to the same scale as the Arch model for height comparison.

In 1993 Jay Tschetter completed a brick mural entitled "Pioneers of Light" for the façade of the Odyssey Theatre (opposite page, top left), which depicts twelve photographers of the 19th-century American West who were instrumental in forming historical perceptions of the landscape and the era. The theatre itself is the only large screen format presentation within the boundaries of a National Park site. Since its opening, existing large format films such as "The Great American West" and "Lewis and Clark: Great Journey West" have been shown there.

An enlarged Museum Store (opposite page, bottom right) and the Levee Mercantile (opposite page, bottom left), a reproduction of an 1870s St. Louis emporium with authentic goods and foods, are administered by Jefferson National Parks Association. These stores are seen as adjuncts to the public programs given within the park, and sell only items tied in with the themes

of the site. In this way a visitor making a purchase takes home educational items that continue to provide information about Jefferson National Expansion Memorial.

All tickets for the films, rides to the top of the Arch, and riverboat cruises are collected at the ticket center, run by Metro (opposite page, top left). The observation deck at the top of the Arch hosts nearly 1 million visitors a year (top right). On a clear day a visitor can see about 30 miles to the west into Missouri and an equal distance into Illinois on the east.

"From its beginning, the Jefferson National Expansion Memorial project broke new ground regarding the relationships of a municipality with the federal government and the notion of a city-government partnership."

- *Robert Blackburn, Administrative Assistant to St. Louis Mayor Raymond R. Tucker (oral history interview, November 9, 1994)*

"My concept right from the beginning for the park was that it would be a forest, a simple forest. It would be more like a forest that you would find out on the prairie, which has one or two species in it, and has thousands of a single kind of tree rather than four or five of this and seventeen of those. This was meant to give a wonderful aura of simplicity and a benign quality to go with the majesty of the Arch."

- Dan Kiley
(oral history interview, July 22, 1993)

147

"I was very impressed with the caliber of the workers. They all seemed to me to be exceptionally intelligent and dedicated. I don't think a group of workers has ever been assembled that will be more outstanding than that. I think that is one reason that the safety record was so good. They all knew what they were doing and they went about their business very quietly and they never seemed to have any qualms about the fact that, yes, the two legs were going to meet at the top."

- Sue Ann Wood

(oral history interview, November 10, 1994)

149

"I was and still am very proud to be a part of it. I think it is a nice part of the history of the city of St. Louis, and we need the National Park Service to keep this dream alive."

- Bill Quigley
(oral history interview, October 28, 1995)

"It was conceived as one of the three or four great symbols of our country. In other words, that it would take its place with the Washington Monument, the Lincoln Memorial, and the Statue of Liberty, in reminding adults and children of the historic events of westward expansion."

- Eero Saarinen
(United States Senate Hearing, 1953)

"The Arch is a symbol of St. Louis as the 'Gateway to the West,' but it also stands for the unfettered human spirit, the human heart eternally searching for the achievement of transcendent goals … It reminds us that the same spirit of enterprise, the same courageous advance into the unknown, and the same faith in man's destiny that characterized our ancestors on America's geographical frontier are qualities which are still needed by us today to cope with the enormous problems of modern technological and sociological frontiers."

- George B. Hartzog, Jr.
(St. Louis Post-Dispatch, *June 10, 1962*)

"The Arch is wonderful on a number of different levels. It has a sense of timelessness about it. The stainless steel and simplicity of form give it an otherworldly quality and it's such a perfect expression of a gateway. It is monumental, as it is meant to be, and it's a little bit magic. I'm glad that it took 15 years for them to produce this building, because my father could spend those 15 years working on it, and loving it, and making it better. It is a tragedy that he wasn't here to see it, because he would have been so pleased. It's certainly my favorite work of my father's. Perhaps, because of its timeless quality, it transcends the rest of his work."

- *Susan Saarinen*

156

APPENDIX

Charles Nagle, JNEM Architectural Competition Jury Member, 1947-1948; from a wire recording of a television broadcast on St. Louis station KSD, February 19, 1948, through the kind services of Steve Mueller of St. Louis, page 34

Dick Bowser, Designer of the Arch Tram System; oral history interview conducted by Robert J. Moore, Jr. on October 8, 1993, page 50

Ted Rennison, Engineer, Eero Saarinen and Associates; oral history interview conducted by Don Haake in March and May, 1981, page 58

Joe Jensen, Engineer, Associate Director, National Park Service, from a paper written by Mr. Jensen for JNEM in August 1968, page 61

Russ Knox, Oiler, Crane Operator; oral history interview conducted by Robert J. Moore, Jr. on July 26, 1995, page 63

Fred Morris, Ironworker on the Arch Project; oral history interview conducted by Robert J. Moore, Jr. on October 23, 1997, page 66

Ted Rennison, Engineer, Eero Saarinen and Associates; oral history, conducted by Don Haake in March and May, 1981, page 74

Russ Knox, Oiler, Crane Operator; oral history, conducted by Robert J. Moore, Jr. on July 26, 1995, page 75

Fred Morris, Ironworker on the Arch Project; oral history, conducted by Robert J. Moore, Jr. on October 23, 1997, page 76

Charles Guggenheim, Filmmaker, *Monument to the Dream*; oral history interview conducted by Robert J. Moore, Jr. on April 12, 1995, page 96

Fred Morris, Ironworker on the Arch Project; oral history, conducted by Robert J. Moore, Jr. on October 23, 1997, page 98

Bill Quigley, Crane Operator, PDM; oral history interview conducted by Robert J. Moore, Jr. on October 28, 1995, page 102

PHOTOGRAPHS:

EVERY REASONABLE ATTEMPT HAS BEEN MADE TO IDENTIFY OWNERS OF COPYRIGHT. ERRORS OR OMISSIONS WILL BE CORRECTED IN SUBSEQUENT EDITIONS.

INTRODUCTION

ARTEAGA PHOTOS LTD.
Page 4

COURTESY OF JEFFERSON NATIONAL EXPANSION MEMORIAL ARCHIVES
Photographer Unknown; Page 8

JEFFERSON NATIONAL PARKS ASSOCIATION
Terrell Creative; Page 3 (top 4)

TERRELL CREATIVE
Chad Combs; Page 2, 6, 11
Joseph M. Luman; Page 3 (bottom)

SAINT LOUIS GLOBE-DEMOCRAT ARCHIVES OF THE SAINT LOUIS MERCANTILE LIBRARY AT THE UNIVERSITY OF MISSOURI-SAINT LOUIS
Page 9

CHAPTER 1

ARTEAGA PHOTOS LTD.
Page 18

COURTESY OF JEFFERSON NATIONAL EXPANSION MEMORIAL ARCHIVES
Photographer Unknown; Page 15, 16, 19 (top, bottom), 21 (top), 22, 23 (left, right)

WESTERN HISTORICAL MANUSCRIPT COLLECTION AT THE UNIVERSITY OF MISSOURI-SAINT LOUIS
Photographer Unknown; Page 12, 13 (top, bottom), 17, 20 (left, right), 21 (bottom)

CHAPTER 2

ARTEAGA PHOTOS LTD.
Page 36 (left)

COURTESY OF THE OFFICE OF DAN KILEY
Page 36 (right)

COURTESY OF JEFFERSON NATIONAL EXPANSION MEMORIAL ARCHIVES
Photographer Unknown; Page 24, 25, 26, 27, 28 (bottom left, top right), 29 (top left, bottom right), 30, 31 (left, right), 32 (all), 33 (top, bottom), 37 (top left, bottom right)

CHAPTER 3

ARTEAGA PHOTOS LTD.
Page 44 (bottom left), 47, 53

DAYTONA BEACH NEWS-JOURNAL
Rick de Yampert; Page 50

COURTESY OF JEFFERSON NATIONAL EXPANSION MEMORIAL ARCHIVES
Photographer Unknown; Page 43, 51 (top right, bottom right)
Ted Rennison; Page 39 (right), 46 (bottom left)
Arteaga Photos Ltd.; Page 49 (all)

SAINT LOUIS GLOBE-DEMOCRAT ARCHIVES OF THE SAINT LOUIS MERCANTILE LIBRARY AT THE UNIVERSITY OF MISSOURI-SAINT LOUIS
Page 39 (left), 51 (left)

© MICHAEL WEITNAUER/GREATBUILDINGS.COM
Page 41 (top)

© NOWITZ/FOLIO, INC.
Page 41 (bottom)

WESTERN HISTORICAL MANUSCRIPT COLLECTION AT THE UNIVERSITY OF MISSOURI-SAINT LOUIS
Arthur Witman; Page 45 (all), 52

COURTESY OF SEVERUD ASSOCIATES
Page 46 (top right)

TERRELL CREATIVE
Joseph M. Luman; Page 38

CHAPTER 4

ARTEAGA PHOTOS LTD.
Page 54, 55 (top left, bottom center), 56 (bottom left), 58 (left, right), 59 (all), 60 (bottom center), 62 (top right, bottom right), 63, 64, 65, 67 (right top, right middle), 69 (top right)

COURTESY OF JEFFERSON NATIONAL EXPANSION MEMORIAL ARCHIVES
Photographer Unknown; Page 67 (top left)
Ted Rennison; Page 60 (top left)
Army Mobility Command; Page 60 (top right)
Gift of E. Coautroman; Page 61

SAINT LOUIS GLOBE-DEMOCRAT ARCHIVES OF THE SAINT LOUIS MERCANTILE LIBRARY AT THE UNIVERSITY OF MISSOURI-SAINT LOUIS
Page 56 (top left)

WESTERN HISTORICAL MANUSCRIPT COLLECTION AT THE UNIVERSITY OF MISSOURI-SAINT LOUIS
Arthur Witman; Page 55 (top right), 56 (top right), 57 (left, right), 62 (top left), 66, 67 (bottom right), 68, 69 (bottom left)

CHAPTER 5

ARTEAGA PHOTOS LTD.
Page 70, 71 (bottom right), 72 (bottom left, top right), 73, 75 (top, bottom), 77 (bottom right), 78, 79, 81, 82 (right), 83 (left, right), 84 (left), 85, 88 (right)

COURTESY OF JEFFERSON NATIONAL EXPANSION MEMORIAL ARCHIVES
Photographer Unknown; Page 74 (left), 77 (bottom left), 87 (right)
Arteaga Photos Ltd.; Page 77 (top left)

WESTERN HISTORICAL MANUSCRIPT COLLECTION AT THE UNIVERSITY OF MISSOURI-SAINT LOUIS
Arthur Witman; Page 71 (top left), 74 (right), 76, 82 (left), 84 (right), 86 (left, right), 87 (left), 88 (left), 89

CHAPTER 6

ARTEAGA PHOTOS LTD.
Page 93, 95, 98, 102 (all), 103 (left), 104 (left), 105, 106 (top left), 107 (top left), 108, 109 (left, right), 112, 113, 117 (right)

© GUGGENHEIM PRODUCTIONS INC.
FOUR-TIME ACADEMY AWARD® WINNER CHARLES GUGGENHEIM filming *MONUMENT TO THE DREAM* IN 1968
Page 96, 97 (top, bottom)

COURTESY OF JEFFERSON NATIONAL EXPANSION MEMORIAL ARCHIVES
Photographer Unknown; Page 91 (left), 100 (bottom left), 107 (right), 110
Ted Rennison; Page 99 (bottom right)

COURTESY OF SUE ANN WOOD
Page 100 (top right)

WESTERN HISTORICAL MANUSCRIPT COLLECTION AT THE UNIVERSITY OF MISSOURI-SAINT LOUIS
Arthur Witman; Page 90, 91 (right), 94, 99 (top, bottom left, bottom center), 101, 103 (right), 104 (right), 106 (bottom left, right), 107 (middle), 111, 114 (left, right), 115 (all), 116 (left, right), 117 (left)

CHAPTER 7

ARTEAGA PHOTOS LTD.
Page 123, 126 (bottom left, top right), 127 (left)

COURTESY OF JEFFERSON NATIONAL EXPANSION MEMORIAL ARCHIVES
Photographer Unknown; Page 130 (top left, bottom left, bottom right), 131 (top left, top right)
Arteaga Photos Ltd.; Page 128 (bottom left), 129 (top left)
Al Bilger; Page 127 (right)
Cecil W. Stoughton; Page 130 (top right), 131 (bottom left)

JEFFERSON NATIONAL PARKS ASSOCIATION
Terrell Creative; Page 125, 128 (right), 129 (top right, bottom right)

WESTERN HISTORICAL MANUSCRIPT COLLECTION AT THE UNIVERSITY OF MISSOURI-SAINT LOUIS
Arthur Witman; Page 118, 119, 120 (all), 121 (all), 122 (all)

CHAPTER 8

ARTEAGA PHOTOS LTD.
Page 132, 135, 136, 137, 142 (bottom left),151,157

DAISUKE HIROTA/IMPACT PHOTOGRAPHICS
Page 140 (bottom left), 153

COURTESY OF JEFFERSON NATIONAL EXPANSION MEMORIAL ARCHIVES
N. G. Messinger; Page 138 (bottom left)
Al Bilger; Page 149 (left)